My Aunties' Recipes

A Love Letter Written in Food

A FAMILY COOKBOOK

Antoinette Jarrett

MY AUNTIES' RECIPES
Copyright © 2024 Antoinette Jarrett

All rights reserved. This book or any portion thereof may not be reproduced, distributed, or transmitted in any form or by any means, including photocopying, recording, or other electronic or mechanical methods, without the express written permission of the publisher except in the case of brief quotations embodied in critical reviews and certain other noncommercial uses permitted by copyright law. For permissions requests, write to the publisher, addressed "Attention: Permissions Coordinator," at the address below.

Printed in the United States of America
ISBN: 978-1-953497-97-0 (Hardcover)
ISBN: 978-1-953497-98-7 (Digital)

Library of Congress Control Number: 2024904408

Published by Cocoon to Wings Publishing
7810 Gall Blvd., #311
Zephyrhills, FL 33541
www.CocoontoWingsBooks.com
(813) 906-WING (9464)

Cover design by ETP Creative

My Aunties' Recipes
A Love Letter Written in Food

THIS IS FOR:

**THE CREATOR
MY FAMILY
EVERYBODY**

> *"Child, people start loving or hating your food long before they taste it. People eat with their eyes. Make sure your plate has some variety, not too saucy or brown or dry. Make sure it looks as good as it tastes."* **—Mom**

MY AUNTIES' RECIPES

My Aunties' Recipes started with the announcement that one of our own was bringing home a bride. What great news! At the time, the pandemic gave birth to a certain amount of craziness and creativity. Instantly, the idea for this love letter took on a life of its own, and it was decided this would be a wonderful way for us to welcome her and others into our family's kitchen.

Aunties are beloved in every culture around the world. We have earned it. Perhaps we hover a little too much and ask too many questions. Yet we're also the ones under the bus with you making sure you are good. What we mean to say, in life as well as the kitchen, is, "Baby, you're doing great. You've got this!"

Explore making all or some of these dishes to test your cooking level and skills. As you discover each recipe, you will find a "Make it Your Own!" section where you can write down how you improvised and made the recipe your own. Aunt Carolyn would tell you, "Stick to the recipe. Stop all that improvising!" The rest of your Aunties will tell you, "Don't be scared!" Cooking is an expressive art form that allows you to use your culinary tools as your paintbrush and the foods as your canvas. Who knows! You may create a masterpiece that you can pass down to the generations coming after you, and when you do, wrap up a piece in some tin foil or a napkin and bring it by so the Aunties can get a taste.

TABLE OF
Contents

Appetizers　12

Pearl's Salmon Party Ball; Chex Trail Mix; Charcuterie Board; Auntie's 7 Layer Dip; Mango Salsa (Vegan); Spinach Dip (Vegetarian); Sticky Asian Sesame Wings; Baked Stuffed Mushrooms (Vegetarian); Bright and Sunny Shrimp Salad; Hummus (Vegan); Sweet and Sour Meatballs

Salads and Soups　30

Cucumber and Tomato Salad; Balenca's Fruit Salad; Corn and Bean Salad with Tarragon; Spinach and Pomegranate Salad; Italian Tomato Salad; Asian Ribeye and Arugula Salad; Vermicelli Salad; Buttermilk Salad; Snow-Day Baked Potato Soup; Homemade Chicken Noodle Soup; Tee's Sausage Potato and Kale Soup

Sauces and Vinaigrettes　46

Best and Basic Vinaigrette; Citrus Vinaigrette; Daddy's Barbecue Sauce; Homemade Gravy; Homemade Blue Cheese Dressing

Entrées　54

"Classic Weekend" Carnitas; South of the Border Stuffed Bell Peppers (Vegetarian); The 3-in-1 Holiday Essential; Easy Chicken Enchiladas; Mississippi Pot Roast; Wade's Classic Sunday Pot Roast; MiMi's Sure-To-Please Pot Roast; Gabby's Sweet Chili Glazed Salmon; White Fish in Cream Sauce; (The "Company Fish"); Egg Rolls in a Bowl; (Low carb); N.O.L.A. Style Red Beans and Rice;

Entrées 54

Gabby's Chicken Fried Rice; Braised Short Ribs in Dark Beer Sauce; BBQ Kabobs; Italian Stuffed Chicken with an Herb Cream Sauce; Quesadillas - Bean and Cheese; Quesadillas - Spinach and Mushrooms; Mediterranean Baked Chicken; Quick Meatloaf; Classic Sunday Meatloaf; Homemade Pizza; Hot Italian Sausage and Pasta; Annie's Perfectly Fried Chicken

Vegetables and Sides 92

AJ's Sautéed Spinach; (Vegetarian); Uncle Jay's Scalloped Potatoes; Mango-Brown Sugar Glazed Sweet Potatoes; Friend's Shaved Cajun Brussels Sprouts (Vegan); Roasted Brussel Sprouts with Bacon; Kidney Beans; Roasted Zucchini and Summer Squash Mix; White Beans with Pancetta; Garlic Cheese Grits; Aunt Balenca's Collard Green Hack; Sautéed Mushrooms; Turnip Greens; Carolyn's Southern Potato Salad

Desserts 110

Pearl's Peach Cobbler; Sour Cream Pound Cake; Lemon Poppy Seed Pound Cake; Toni's Magic Margarita Cheesecake; Auntie Nette's Orange Pound Cake; 5-Star Classic Coconut Cake; Kick-To-The-Head Chocolate Cake; Toni's Sweet Potato Pie; Red Velvet Cake; 7UP Pound Cake; Lemon Bars; Classic Sweet Potato Pie; Red Velvet Cake – The Original Family Recipe; Holiday Chocolate Candy with Nuts; Hummingbird Cake; Judy's Carrot Cake; The Ultimate German Chocolate Cake

> *"Want to know the best tool a cook can have? Clean hands."*
> **—Aunt Carolyn**

MEASUREMENTS
REFERENCE CHART

Tablespoons	**Tbsp**
Teaspoons	**tsp**
Ounce	**oz**
Cup	**c**
Pound	**lb**
Quart	**qt**
Package	**pkg**
Approximately	**approx**

APPETIZERS

A CHARCUTERIE BOARD

A LOVE LETTER

My Love,

This family's love affair with food began with our parents knowing how to make ends meet. For years, one of their odd jobs was to work private parties. Dad would bartend, and Mom joined the catering staff for the evening. In the middle of the night, they'd come home with a treasure trove of little bites and tastes. In the wee hours of the morning, school was in session.

Mom and Dad would explain each item and make it somehow approachable to us. One would say, "You see these tiny little black things? This is caviar. It's salty. You only need a little bit." The other would join in, saying, "This, this is pâté; it's nothing but a fancy kind of liver." So, our tiny kitchen became our classroom. It was the beginning of our fascination with food. Out of bits of folded napkins and tin foil, we learned a larger lesson that most things in life are more accessible than they first appear. Wade and Rosie (our parents) did it using food as the medium. They would walk us through the unfamiliar. Some things we loved, others we did not, but after the lesson, we knew more than when it started.

Now, I believe my parents were preparing us to become part of a world they themselves couldn't fully access. In these private homes, our mom and dad were largely unnoticed, not guests but there to provide a service. On some level, they knew we would have better opportunities to enter rooms and sit at tables, which excluded them. They wanted us to recognize what was to come. It was their way of preparing the next generation. So, these sessions were their way of saying, "Baby, be ready."

Salmon Ball

1. Large Can Salmon, drained & deboned.
1. Large 8z Cream Cheese
4 tbsp lemon Juice
2 - 2½ tbsp. grated onions
Salt to taste
1 tsp Horse radish.

Instruction

Soften Cream Cheese, mix all ingredients except Salmon with mixer. Add Salmon and stir till well blended. Put in refrigerator till firm. Shape in ball and roll in snipped parsley.

Pearl's Salmon Party Ball

Mom was a creative, and she loved fish. This appetizer allowed her, in 1970's Alabama, to express a fanciful, refined side of herself and her cooking. She always seemed happy making this appetizer.

MAKE IT YOUR OWN

INGREDIENTS

- 16oz can salmon, drained and deboned
- 8oz cream cheese at room temperature
- 4 Tbsp lemon juice
- 3 Tbsp grated onion
- 2 tsp horseradish
- ¼ tsp salt
- ¼ tsp liquid smoke, be careful, too much is awful
- 3 Tbsp chopped parsley
- ½ c chopped pecans, to garnish

Directions

1. Combine all ingredients except the parsley and pecans. Mix thoroughly, then chill for several hours.
2. Once chilled, shape into a ball and roll the ball in parsley and pecans being sure to cover all sides.
3. Cover with plastic wrap and chill well.
4. Serve alongside chips and/or crackers

Chex Trail Mix

INGREDIENTS

- 2 c Chocolate Chex cereal
- 2 c Rice Chex cereal
- 1 ¼ c raisins
- 1 c M&M's or similar candy
- 1 c peanuts
- 1 c roasted almonds
- ¾ c chocolate chips, milk chocolate

MAKE IT YOUR OWN

Directions

1. In a large mixing bowl, combine all ingredients and gently mix to combine.
2. Eat immediately or seal in an airtight container and store in a cool place.

Charcuterie Board

A charcuterie or grazing board is only limited by your imagination. Typically, the board is made up of cured meat, cheeses, breads, vegetables, nuts, and fruit. There is no pattern to the display, but symmetry is crucial. There is never a perfect board. Each is as individual as what you have on hand in the kitchen on any given day. Here is a sample list to get you started. Adjust the ingredients based on how many people you want to serve.

INGREDIENTS

- ¼ lb apricot cheese
- An assortment of breads and crackers
- ¼ lb seedless green grapes
- ¼ lb seedless red grapes
- 1 stone fruit, thinly sliced
- An assortment of nuts
- A variety of condiments

INGREDIENTS

- ¼ lb Cajun turkey deli meat, thinly sliced
- ¼ lb Honey-baked ham
- ¼ lb salami
- ¼ lb prosciutto
- ¼ lb extra sharp cheddar cheese
- ¼ lb Havarti cheese with dill

Directions

1. Using a decorative tray or cutting board, start by placing the meats in a symmetrical pattern. Fold some, roll some, pile some, stack some.
2. Next, add the three cheeses and other ingredients to fill in the empty spaces.
3. Serve immediately or cover and place in the fridge until ready to serve.

Auntie's 7 Layer Dip

INGREDIENTS

- 2 cans bean dip, heated and allowed to cool
- 2 c guacamole
- 2 c sour cream
- 2 Tbsp taco seasoning
- 2 c Mexican-style shredded cheese
- 1 c tomatoes, diced and deseeded
- ½ c green onions, chopped
- ½ c pickled jalapeños, drained and chopped
- 1 bag Fritos corn chips

MAKE IT YOUR OWN

Directions

1. Use a large, clear serving dish. Spread a layer of bean dip.
2. Top with guacamole.
3. Thoroughly mix sour cream and taco seasoning then spread over guacamole.
4. Sprinkle on the cheese.
5. Add tomatoes.
6. Top with onions and jalapeños.
7. Serve along with corn chips.

Mango Salsa (Vegan)

A great host always ensures each guest, no matter their dietary preferences, has something they will eat and enjoy.

INGREDIENTS

- 2 c fresh, ripe mango, evenly diced
- 2 Tbsp fresh lime juice
- 1 Serrano pepper, seeds removed and finely chopped
- 1 clove fresh garlic, minced
- 1/4 red onion, finely diced

MAKE IT YOUR OWN

Directions

1. Combine all ingredients and refrigerate for at least one hour before serving.
2. Serve with vegetables or tortilla chips

Spinach Dip (Vegetarian)

INGREDIENTS

- 1 pkg frozen chopped spinach, thaw, drain, then squeeze to remove excess water
- 1 pkg Knorr Vegetable Soup Mix
- 1 pint sour cream
- 1 c real mayonnaise
- 3 green onions, finely chopped

MAKE IT YOUR OWN

_____
_____
_____
_____
_____
_____
_____

Directions

1. Combine all ingredients in a mixing large bowl.
2. Place in refrigerator and chill for at least an hour.
3. Place in a serving bowl and serve along with tortilla chips or toast points.

Sticky Asian Sesame Wings

INGREDIENTS

- 1 lb chicken drumettes, thawed
- 1 Tbsp Tony Chachere's seasoning
- 1/2 tsp salt
- 1/2 tsp garlic powder
- 1/2 tsp garlic salt
- 1/2 tsp black pepper
- 1/2 tsp smoked paprika
- 1/2 tsp onion powder
- 1 Tbsp all-purpose flour
- 1/2 Tbsp corn starch
- 2 Tbsp avocado oil

SAUCE

- 1/3 c honey
- 1/4 c soy sauce
- 2 Tbsp Asian chili sauce
- 2 cloves fresh garlic, minced
- 1 tsp ginger paste
- 1 Tbsp rice vinegar
- Juice of 1 large lime
- 1 Tbsp brown sugar
- 1 Tbsp sesame seeds
- green onion, diced to garnish (optional)

Directions

1. Preheat oven to 350°F.
2. Remove the chicken from the package and rinse under cool water. Pat dry with paper towels and place the chicken in a large sealable plastic bag.
3. In a small mixing bowl, combine the Tony Chachere's seasoning, salt, garlic powder, garlic salt, black pepper, smoked paprika, and onion powder. Mix well.
4. Sprinkle approximately 2/3 of the seasoning mixture over the chicken and shake well, being careful to coat all pieces.

Directions

5. In another small mixing bowl, combine flour, cornstarch, and remaining seasoning mixture. Stir well to combine, then add to the plastic bag and shake well to coat all sides.

6. Place coated chicken on a shallow baking sheet with a wire rack and add to the preheated oven.

7. Bake for approximately 35 to 40 minutes, turning pieces about halfway through the cooking time.

8. Once done, remove the drumettes from the oven and allow to cool.

9. Heat a large saucepan over medium heat and combine all ingredients except the sesame seeds and green onions.

10. Mix well to combine and allow the sauce to simmer, approximately 5 to 7 minutes or until the sauce thickens slightly.

11. In a large mixing bowl, add the chicken and pour the sauce over the chicken. Stir or toss to coat the drumettes.

12. Place the chicken on a serving tray and sprinkle with sesame seeds and green onions.

MAKE IT YOUR OWN

Baked Stuffed Mushrooms (Vegetarian)

To clean mushrooms, do not submerge in water. Either brush gently with a vegetable brush or wipe clean with a damp paper towel.

INGREDIENTS

- 18 large mushrooms, cleaned
- 5 medium mushrooms, cleaned
- 2 sticks butter
- 4 cloves fresh garlic, minced
- 1 large onion, minced
- 1 Tbsp fresh parsley
- 2 c Parmesan cheese, grated (on the shelf)
- 1 c seasoned breadcrumbs
- 1/2 tsp sea salt
- 1/2 tsp black pepper
- 1 Tbsp fresh lemon juice

Directions

1. Preheat oven to 350°F.
2. Separate stems from the large mushrooms. Set aside the caps and mince the stems.
3. Mince the caps and stems of the smaller mushrooms.
4. In a large saucepan, melt one stick of butter over medium heat, then add the garlic and sauté for approximately one (1) minute.
5. Add the onions and minced mushrooms. Cook until the mixture looks like oatmeal.
6. Add the parsley and parmesan cheese and fold them into the mushroom mixture.
7. Add the breadcrumbs, salt, pepper, and lemon juice, and fold into the mixture.
8. Remove the pan from the heat. If the mixture is too soft, add a small

amount of breadcrumbs. The mixture should be somewhat stiff.

9. Set aside and allow to cool.
10. With a spoon, add the cooled mixture to the mushroom caps.
11. Melt the second stick of butter in a small pan. Dip the mushroom caps into the melted butter, ladle ample amounts of melted butter over the stuffed caps, then place the caps on a baking sheet.
12. Bake for approximately 10-15 minutes, then turn the pan in the oven and continue baking another 5-10 minutes. Mushrooms are done when they are golden brown and can be pierced easily.

MAKE IT YOUR OWN

_____
_____
_____
_____
_____
_____
_____
_____
_____
_____
_____

Bright and Sunny Shrimp Salad

INGREDIENTS

- 2.5 lbs shrimp, deveined
- 1 Tbsp light-tasting olive oil
- Sea salt and black pepper to taste (approximately 1/2 tsp each to start)
- 1 c premium mayonnaise (not Miracle Whip)
- 1 Tbsp orange zest (approximately 2 oranges). Avoid the white part
- 2 Tbsp fresh orange juice
- 1 Tbsp white wine vinegar
- 1/4 c fresh dill, minced
- 2 Tbsp capers, drained
- 2 Tbsp red onion, finely diced

Directions

1. Preheat oven to 400°F.
2. Wash the shrimp and cut the shell of the shrimp to devein, leaving as much of the shell on the shrimp as possible.
3. Place the shrimp on a baking sheet and pat them dry with paper towels.
4. Drizzle the shrimp with olive oil and sprinkle with salt and pepper.
5. Toss the shrimp, then spread them on a baking sheet in a single layer.
6. Roast the shrimp in the oven for approximately 5-7 minutes until the shells are just pink, the texture has firmed, and the shrimp is cooked through.
7. Remove from the oven and allow to cool for about 5 minutes.
8. In a large mixing bowl, make the sauce by whisking together mayonnaise, orange zest, orange juice, vinegar, and a bit of salt and pepper.
9. When the shrimp is cool, remove all the shells and roughly chop, if desired, or leave whole. You decide! Then toss the shrimp in the sauce.
10. Add the dill, capers, and onions. Toss well.
11. Let the salad sit at room temperature for about 30 minutes, then serve.

12. If you are making ahead, cover the salad, chill in the refrigerator, and then serve at room temperature. If making ahead, you may have to add a small amount of additional mayonnaise to return to the right consistency.

13. Serve with a simply flavored cracker.

> *"If you understand what they eat, then you understand who they are."* **—Auntie Nette**

MAKE IT YOUR OWN

_____
_____
_____
_____
_____
_____
_____
_____
_____
_____
_____
_____

Hummus (Vegan)

The following is a classic recipe for hummus, a healthy dip that can be easily changed to suit your tastes or what's available in your kitchen. For a new dip, try adding roasted red peppers to the following recipe. Other flavors that work well are - roasted garlic, chipotle, etc. Create something you love.

INGREDIENTS

- 1 can chickpeas, drained
- 1/3 c tahini
- 1 small clove garlic
- Juice from 1 large lemon
- 1 ice cube
- kosher salt to taste
- Olive oil
- A sprinkle of smoked paprika, optional

Directions

1. In a blender, add chickpeas and blend into a powdery paste.
2. Add tahini, garlic, lemon juice, ice cube, and salt. Blend for approximately one (1) minute then slowly start adding oil.
3. Continue adding oil and processing for approximately 2-3 minutes longer.
4. Once the hummus reaches the right consistency, taste and adjust salt and oil if needed.
5. Add the hummus to a serving bowl, drizzle with an additional amount of olive oil to finish, and a sprinkle of paprika, if desired.

MAKE IT YOUR OWN

Sweet and Sour Meatballs

MEATBALLS

- 2 lbs ground beef
- 1 pkg Lipton Onion Soup Mix
- 1/2 c breadcrumbs
- Salt and pepper to taste

SAUCE

- 1 c ketchup
- 1 1/2 c apricot nectar
- 2 Tbsp horseradish
- 2 Tbsp yellow mustard
- 3/4 c brown sugar
- 1/2 c white vinegar

MAKE IT YOUR OWN

Directions

1. Preheat oven to 400°F.
2. In a large mixing bowl, mix together the soup mix, ground beef, breadcrumbs, salt, and pepper.
3. Use a spoon or scoop to make small meatballs and place them on a cookie sheet.
4. Brown the meatballs until done, approximately 20 minutes. Remove from the oven, allow to cool slightly, and then drain on a paper towel.
5. Meanwhile, combine ketchup, apricot nectar, horseradish, mustard, brown sugar, and vinegar in a medium saucepan. Stir to combine and simmer for approximately 10 - 15 minutes.
6. Add the meatballs to the sauce, then gently stir to cover completely. Pour into a large serving bowl.

Have a small container of toothpicks handy.

SALADS AND SOUPS

SAUSAGE POTATO AND KALE SOUP

A LOVE LETTER

My Love,

It's amazing that something as simple as a bowl of soup can call to mind memories of people, time, and even emotions from long ago. For me, a real foodie, a simple bowl of potato soup is ranked as one of the greatest meals of my life. Every time I make it, it takes me back to one day of childhood.

With my parents always working, it was rare for everyone in the family to be together for unscheduled days on end. However, one year, Birmingham, Alabama received the gift of a winter storm. Roads were closed, schools were canceled and as an elementary school student, nothing was as welcomed as a snow day!

We bundled up, found makeshift sleds and for hours road the hill that ran in front of our house. It was exhausting. It was perfect. I remember coming in famished and sitting down to a delicious bowl of my mother's soup. A few years ago, just before she passed, I recalled this special memory to mom and was shocked she had no recollection of it ---at all! Eager to help Mom recall such an important meal; I described it in great detail hoping to spark a memory. Still nothing. Finally, Mom dismissed the deep dive down memory lane in her typical, practical way saying, "Child, I was just trying to feed all of y'all."

Cucumber and Tomato Salad

INGREDIENTS

- 1 large cucumber
- 1 ½ c cherry tomatoes
- ¼ c red onion, thinly sliced
- ½ c Best Vinaigrette (recipe included in the Sauce and Vinaigrettes section)
- ½ tsp sugar
- Salt and pepper to taste

MAKE IT YOUR OWN

Directions

1. Wash cucumber and tomatoes. Pat dry.
2. With a vegetable peeler, remove alternating strips of skin from the cucumber. Cut vertically, then into ½" slices.
3. Halve tomatoes vertically and deseed.
4. In a large mixing bowl, mix cucumber, tomatoes, onions, vinaigrette, and sugar.
5. Taste. Add salt and pepper.
6. Mix thoroughly to coat vegetables with dressing.
7. Place in the fridge until ready to serve.
8. Serve using a slotted spoon to avoid the salad being overdressed.

Balenca's Fruit Salad

This recipe is completely scalable. Add as much or as little of the ingredients as you like.

INGREDIENTS
• Blueberries
• Mandarin oranges
• Pineapples, chunks
• Strawberries, halved
• Poppy seed salad dressing
• Crushed nuts
• Bananas, sliced to garnish
• Whipped cream

Cook's Tips

Always err on the side of less-is-more when dressing a salad. Avoid overdressing!

Directions

1. In a large bowl, combine all fruit except bananas.
2. Drizzle with poppy seed dressing to taste.
3. Sprinkle in crushed nuts.
4. Top individual servings with banana slices and whipped cream.

MAKE IT YOUR OWN
_____
_____
_____
_____
_____
_____
_____
_____
_____
_____

Corn and Bean Salad with Tarragon

INGREDIENTS

- 2 c fresh green beans, halved
- 1 c fresh or canned yellow wax beans, halved
- 6 ears of fresh white corn kernels
- 1 c chopped red bell pepper
- 1/2 c finely chopped red onion
- 1/4 c white wine vinegar
- 1/4 c Dijon mustard
- 2 Tbsp chopped fresh tarragon
- 2 garlic cloves
- 1/2 c canola oil
- 1/4 c "light tasting "olive oil

MAKE IT YOUR OWN

Directions

1. Cook green and yellow beans in a large pot of boiling salted water for about 4 minutes. Drain and shock the beans by submerging them in iced water. Drain and pat dry.
2. Mix all vegetables in a large bowl. Cover and refrigerate.
3. Blend vinegar, mustard, tarragon, and garlic. Slowly add olive and canola oils. Salt and pepper to taste.
4. Coat vegetables with the dressing.
5. Cool or serve at room temperature.

Spinach and Pomegranate Salad

INGREDIENTS

- 6 c spinach leaves, torn
- 1 small avocado, sliced thin
- Seeds of 1 medium pomegranate
- ¾ c Balsamic dressing (or to taste)

MAKE IT YOUR OWN

Directions

1. Wash and pat dry the spinach leaves. Tear them and add them to a large, shallow bowl.
2. Arrange avocado slices over spinach.
3. Add pomegranate seeds.
4. Add balsamic dressing.
5. Serve either chilled or at room temperature.

Italian Tomato Salad

Make ahead. The longer the flavors get to "marry," the more delicious it becomes. Serve as a salad, side dish, or as a topping on bruschetta. Then, serve the next day in a whole different way. Feeds a crowd.

INGREDIENTS

- 8-10 #4664 tomatoes on the vine
- 1-2 garlic cloves
- Black pepper (coarsely ground)
- McCormick Italian seasoning
- 5 Tbsp fresh oregano
- Good Seasons Italian Dressing
- ½ c "light tasting" olive oil
- ⅓ c white wine vinegar
- 3 Tbsp water

Directions

1. Wash and pat dry the tomatoes. On a cutting board, halve, quarter, then quarter tomatoes again, almost like an orange. Place the cut tomatoes on an aluminum foil pan lined with paper towels. Remove and discard juice, seeds, and white veins. Pile tomatoes into a large, shallow bowl. Rinse the cutting board.
2. Slice the garlic cloves super thin.
3. 1 ½ tsp black pepper for a large bowl.
4. 1 ½ tsp Italian seasoning for a large bowl.
5. Chop fresh oregano.
6. Purchase the Italian dressing with the cruet. Make according to the package recipe. Put it in the fridge to thicken.
7. Shake on the dressing. Be careful not to overdress – use approximately half the bottle.

Asian Ribeye and Arugula Salad

INGREDIENTS

- 2 Tbsp toasted sesame oil
- 2 Tbsp extra virgin olive oil (1 tbsp for marinade, 1 for searing)
- 2 Tbsp soy sauce
- 4 cloves of fresh garlic, minced
- 2 Tbsp fresh ginger, minced
- ¼ c fresh lime juice
- 4 c arugula (rinsed and dried)
- Adobo seasoning and black pepper to taste
- Lemon zest

Directions

1. Thinly slice the steak while partially frozen. The thinner it is sliced, the faster the cook time. After slicing, let it rest until it reaches room temperature. Rinse the beef and pat it dry. Sprinkle with Adobo and pepper to taste.
2. Make the dressing in a small bowl by combining sesame oil, olive oil, soy, garlic, ginger, and lime juice. Set aside. Chill or allow to sit at room temperature.
3. Heat the rest of the oil in a heavy skillet (use cast iron if possible). Oil should be hot.
4. Add the beef to the skillet and stir continuously until done. Approximately 3-5 minutes. Remove the beef from the heat one step below your preference. Let steak rest.
5. Arrange the arugula on serving plates. Arrange the rested steak atop the greens.
6. Remix the dressing and drizzle it lightly over the salad.
7. Garnish with lemon zest.

Recipe Tips

1. Know your cuts of steak. Sirloin is super lean with tight muscle fibers. A ribeye is full of marbling (streaks of fat), which gives it flavor.
2. Cuts of meat with a bone are more flavorful but take longer to cook.
3. When cooking steak, remove just before done to your liking. If you like well done, stop cooking at medium. Remember, residual heat will continue cooking food after it is removed from the heat.

Vermicelli Salad

INGREDIENTS

- 1 lb shrimp (preferably cleaned with shells on)
- 1 16oz package vermicelli
- 1 Tbsp Ac'cent Flavor Enhancer
- 1 Tbsp Lawry's Salt
- 3 Tbsp Lemon Juice
- 4 Tbsp Wesson oil
- 1 4oz can diced pimento drained
- 3/4 c chopped onion
- 1 c chopped green, yellow, orange, and/or red bell pepper
- 1 small can chopped ripe olives
- 2 c diced celery
- ¼ c capers
- 1.5 c Hellmann's mayo
- PAM cooking spray

MAKE IT YOUR OWN

Directions

1. Cook pasta (do not overcook), cool, rinse, and drain.
2. Mix together Ac'cent, season salt, lemon juice, and oil.
3. Toss the mixture over the cooked pasta, cover, and marinate at least overnight in the fridge (the longer the better).
4. Preheat oven to 325°F.
5. Spray a shallow baking sheet with cooking spray.
6. Place shrimp in a single layer and cook until just done, approximately. 20 minutes.
7. Cool shrimp. Remove shells and roughly chop the shrimp. Add them to an extra-large mixing bowl.
8. Add pimentos, onion, bell pepper, olives, celery, capers, and mayonnaise to the shrimp.
9. Add the marinated pasta then toss thoroughly to combine.

    Serve immediately or return to fridge.

Cook's Tips

1. Any mayo-based dish will spoil easily. The same is true for dishes with eggs and onion. Always keep them refrigerated and within a safe temperature zone.

Recommended temperature zones

1. Cold foods: the food-safe temperature is 40°F and below.

    Hot foods: the food-safe temperature is 140°F and above

Buttermilk Salad

This recipe is an old family favorite passed on by my mother. It was originally given to her by her very best friend, Mrs. Dorothy Perdue. Any time I have prepared this salad and taken it to work, church gatherings, etc., it has always been a hit with everyone.
–Aunt Carolyn

INGREDIENTS

- 8oz can crushed pineapples, undrained
- 2 c buttermilk, chilled
- 1 16oz tub Cool Whip
- 1 c chopped nuts
- 1 large box Strawberry Jell-O

Directions

1. Heat pineapples with juice and Jell-O to a boil in a heavy saucepan over medium heat. Remove from the heat just after the pineapple mixture reaches a boil.
2. Set aside and refrigerate for 20 to 30 minutes.
3. Once cool, add the buttermilk to the pineapple mixture and stir thoroughly.
4. Fold in Cool Whip, then stir until it is lump-free.
5. Mix in nuts.
6. Set in a mold and refrigerate overnight.

    Unmold, then garnish with more nuts if desired.

MAKE IT YOUR OWN

Snow-Day Baked Potato Soup

INGREDIENTS

- 5 large baking potatoes, baked
- 1/3 c. butter or margarine
- 1 large onion, chopped
- 1/3 c all-purpose flour
- 1 quart heavy cream
- 3 cups whole milk
- 2 tsp salt
- 1/2 tsp ground white pepper
- 2 cups (8 ounces) shredded Cheddar cheese
- 8 bacon slices, cooked and crumbled, for garnish
- Chives, for garnish

Directions

1. Remove peels and slightly mash potatoes with a potato masher.
2. In a large, heavy pot, melt the butter over medium heat.
3. Add onion, and sauté until tender.
4. Sprinkle in flour and stir continuously until smooth.
5. Add potatoes, heavy cream, milk, salt, and pepper.
6. Cook over low heat for about 30 minutes.
7. Garnish with remaining ingredients or as desired.

MAKE IT YOUR OWN

> "It's so much easier if you clean up as you go." —**Aunt Jacqui**

Homemade Chicken Noodle Soup

INGREDIENTS

- 1 whole chicken
- 8 c chicken stock
- 2 tbsp olive oil
- 1 medium white onion, peeled and diced
- 6 garlic cloves, minced
- 1 parsnip, peeled and chopped
- 3 medium carrots, peeled and diced
- 3 stalks celery, trimmed and diced (ends removed)
- Rosemary, 3 sprigs
- Thyme, 3 sprigs
- Sage, 1 sprig
- ½ pack wide egg noodles
- Salt and pepper to taste
- ½ c parsley, chopped
- ⅓ c basil, finely chopped
- 1 can cream of chicken soup (optional to thicken)

Directions

1. Remove the giblets from the chicken cavity. Rinse the chicken, pat dry, salt and pepper liberally. Set aside.
2. In a heavy pot, add oil and allow to heat up. Add onions and cook until slightly translucent. Add garlic just before done. Continue stirring and cook through approximately another 2 minutes. Remove from the heat.
3. Add seasoned chicken and stock. Cover and cook over medium heat until done, approximately 65 minutes.
4. Once the chicken is done, remove the pot from the heat and the chicken from the pot. Retain liquid!
5. Separate meat and retain. Discard the bones and skin, paying attention to the small, fine bones along the back. Shred the chicken and return it to the pot. Add 1 can of cream of chicken soup if desired. Taste and adjust seasonings if needed.

6. Add parsnip, carrots, celery, and noodles to the broth. Cover and simmer on low for approximately 15 minutes.
7. In the last 5 minutes of cooking, add the additional herbs.

Cook's Tip

1. If you cannot access fresh herbs, the rule of thumb in substituting dried for fresh herbs is usually 1 tsp of dried to 1 tbsp of fresh.

MAKE IT YOUR OWN

Tee's Sausage Potato and Kale Soup

INGREDIENTS

- 1 lb Owens Country sausage
- 4-6 russet potatoes, cubed
- 1 onion, chopped
- 4 cloves garlic, pureed
- 5 chicken bouillon cubes
- 40 ounces chicken broth
- 1 bunch kale, stems removed and cut into small pieces
- 1 c heavy whipping cream
- 2 Tbsp flour
- Salt and black pepper to taste
- Cayenne pepper to taste
- 1 lb. bacon, cooked and crumbled
- ½ tsp red pepper, crushed
- Water

Directions

1. Brown the sausage in a sauté pan with the red pepper.
2. In a slow cooker, add sausage, potatoes, onions, garlic, chicken broth, salt, pepper, and cayenne. Add enough water to cover the vegetables and meat.
3. Cook on high for 3-4 hours (or low for 5-6 hours) until potatoes are soft.
4. Half an hour before serving, mix the flour into the cream until lump-free.
5. Add cream and kale to the crock pot and stir. Cook on high for 30 minutes or until thickened.
6. Garnish with bacon and chives, then serve immediately.

MAKE IT YOUR OWN

SAUCES AND VINAIGRETTES

VINAIGRETTES

A LOVE LETTER

My Love,

The small things matter, especially in the kitchen. When time is your greatest gift, don't be afraid of taking a shortcut. Uncle Wade was known for great barbecue and even greater barbecue sauce! Because he was always productive but short on time, he bought bottled barbecue sauce and "doctored" it. Then he perfected it. To this day, whenever I taste it, the sauce transports me back to lightning bugs, R&B hits, and laughter, lots of laughter.

This hardworking man would spend just a little bit of time changing something familiar into something pretty extraordinary. In doing so, he made an indelible mark on the whole family.

Best and Basic Vinaigrette

INGREDIENTS

- ¼ c "light tasting" olive oil
- ½ c Alessi white wine vinegar
- 2 tsp Morton "Nature's Seasons" seasoning blend

MAKE IT YOUR OWN

_____
_____
_____
_____
_____
_____
_____

Directions

1. Mix all ingredients together in a well-sealed cruet and shake vigorously.
2. Serve immediately.

Citrus Vinaigrette

INGREDIENTS

- ½ small shallot, minced
- 1 ¼ Tbsp fresh squeezed lemon juice
- 3 Tbsp orange juice, freshly squeezed if possible
- ½ c "light tasting" olive oil
- ¼ c Alessi white wine or champagne vinegar
- ½ Tbsp sugar
- ½ tsp salt, or to taste
- ¼ tsp black pepper, or to taste

MAKE IT YOUR OWN

Directions

1. Mix all ingredients together in a well-sealed cruet and shake vigorously.
2. Serve immediately.

Daddy's Barbecue Sauce

INGREDIENTS

- 1 bottle of your favorite barbecue sauce
- ½ c ketchup
- ½ stick butter (4 tbsp)
- 2 Tbsp brown sugar
- 2 Tbsp Worcestershire sauce
- 2 Tbsp liquid smoke
- 2 tsp yellow mustard
- 2 lemons squeezed for juice
- Rind from half a lemon

MAKE IT YOUR OWN

Directions

1. Combine all ingredients together in a heavy saucepan.
2. Cook over medium-low heat, stirring often. Cook until sauce reduces (thickens slightly). Approximately 30 minutes.
3. Allow to cool and remove lemon rinds. Serve or store in the refrigerator.

Homemade Gravy

Scale this recipe to make as much or as little gravy as you'd like. When changing the quantity, just remember to use equal parts of fat and flour.

INGREDIENTS

- ¼ c pan drippings
- ¼ c all-purpose flour
- 3-4 c of liquid, i.e., water, stock, milk, etc.
- Salt and pepper, to taste

Directions

1. After cooking your meat by roasting, frying, etc., remove the meat from the pan and pour off all the fat except ¼ cup.
2. Take a spoon or spatula and scrape the bottom of the pan to loosen all the bits from the bottom. Leave them in the pan! This is your flavor.
3. Over medium-low heat, allow the drippings to heat and sprinkle in flour. With a wire whisk, quickly stir the flour to dissolve. Continue stirring until it is brown and the consistency of a well-baked potato. This is called the roux. Remember, your gravy will be the color of the roux as a general rule unless you're making a gravy with milk or cream. Err on the side of cooking it longer than you'd think. Shoot for a nutty, brown color.
4. Whisk continuously and slowly add the liquid. Continue stirring until the liquid is completely incorporated and the gravy is free of lumps.
5. Taste and add salt and pepper to taste.
6. Simmer to thicken the gravy and serve immediately.

MAKE IT YOUR OWN

_____
_____
_____
_____
_____
_____
_____

Homemade Blue Cheese Dressing

INGREDIENTS

- 2 ½ oz blue cheese
- 3 Tbsp buttermilk
- 3 Tbsp sour cream
- 2 Tbsp mayonnaise
- 2 tsp white wine vinegar
- ¼ tsp white sugar
- ¼ tsp garlic powder
- Salt and pepper to taste

MAKE IT YOUR OWN

Directions

1. In a small mixing bowl, crumble blue cheese, then mash with a fork. Add buttermilk and continue to mix well.
2. Add all ingredients except salt and pepper. Blend well.
3. Add salt and pepper to taste

ENTRÉES

POT ROAST

A LOVE LETTER

My Love,

Take it from me; it doesn't matter how often another cooks; the star of the kitchen is always the one who masters this section. People appreciate great food, but they will celebrate a great entrée. Occasionally, a cut of meat is so exceptional that it outshines the preparer and becomes the star itself. Recently, I was at my favorite supermarket and on display was the most amazing ribcap, the choicest part of a ribeye. I couldn't look away and started quizzing the butcher. He taught as other shoppers joined in, asking questions of their own. Everyone wanted to know how to approach such a thing of beauty.

The butcher's counter was full of excitement and so were the friends who received photos of such an unusual cut. In the kitchen as in life, it takes courage to tackle the unfamiliar. Take the risk and you might just discover a star.

"Classic Weekend" Carnitas

Feeds an army!! This is a recipe for tailgating, family reunions, an open house, or whenever you need to feed a crowd. This pork street taco is a fan favorite!!

INGREDIENTS

- 4-5 lbs. pork shoulder, trim off extra fat
- 1 Tbsp chili powder
- 2 tsp ground cumin
- 2 tsp dried oregano
- 2 Tbsp salt (+/-) to taste
- 1 Tbsp ground black pepper
- 8-9 garlic cloves peeled and crushed
- 2 onions quartered
- 2 oranges, juiced
- 2 limes, juiced
- 1 lemon, juiced
- ¼ c orange juice from concentrate
- 2-3 large packs tortillas (corn or flour) warmed

FOR ASSEMBLY

- Salsa, large
- Onion, large finely diced
- Lime wedges
- Cilantro leaves finely chopped
- Any other toppings you would like – i.e., cheese, sour cream, diced tomatoes, shredded lettuce

Directions

1. In a small bowl, whisk together chili powder, cumin, oregano, salt, and pepper.
2. Rub thoroughly over all sides of the pork.
3. Add pieces of garlic to the crevices of the pork shoulder.
4. Add additional garlic, onions, orange, OJ, lime, lemon juices and rinds.
5. Cover and place in the refrigerator to marinate for several hours or overnight.
6. Remove rinds and place seasoned pork and liquid in the slow cooker.

7. Cover and cook on low for 8 hours or on high for 4 to 5 hours.

8. Remove pork shoulder and shred, then return to the pot with the juices. Taste and add more salt and pepper if needed. Cover and cook for an additional 30 minutes.

9. Heat a small amount of oil on a griddle or in a frying pan. Place tortillas on the oiled surface and warm on both sides.

10. Assemble tacos, adding your choice of toppings.

MAKE IT YOUR OWN

South of the Border Stuffed Bell Peppers (Vegetarian)

INGREDIENTS

- 6 red bell peppers
- 1 can Southwest corn, drained
- 1 can Black beans, drained
- 1 c uncooked rice
- 1 packet of taco seasoning
- 1 c jarred salsa (like Pace or Old El Paso)

TOPPINGS

- Any of your favorite toppings, i.e., shredded cheese, sour cream, guacamole, jalapeño peppers, etc.

MAKE IT YOUR OWN

Directions

1. Preheat the slow cooker to low.
2. Wash and dry your peppers. Cut off the top of the peppers (stem side) and core, removing the seeds and membrane.
3. In a large bowl, mix the remaining ingredients until well combined.
4. Spoon the mixture into the peppers and place the peppers into the slow cooker.
5. Cover the slow cooker with lid and allow the peppers to cook until done, approximately 3-4 hours.
6. Place the cooked peppers onto a serving plate and garnish as desired.

Serving suggestions

- May be served as a vegetarian meal or as a side dish along with your choice of meat.

THE 3-IN-1 HOLIDAY ESSENTIAL:

Roasted Turkey, Cornbread Dressing, and Giblet Gravy

This 3-dish recipe will be the foundation of your holiday table. The combination of turkey, dressing, and giblet gravy covers the basics of a traditional holiday feast. From there, simply add your favorite sides, and you will be set to host the whole family.

INGREDIENTS

- 1 whole turkey, thawed as directed on packaging
- 2 c water
- Several pats of butter for bird
- Salt and pepper to taste for bird
- 1 large skillet of day-old cornbread, about 8 cups
- Salt (to taste)
- 1 Tbsp black pepper
- 1 tsp onion powder

INGREDIENTS

- 1 tsp garlic powder
- 1 tsp smoked paprika
- ½ tsp thyme
- 2 Tbsp ground sage
- 2 Tbsp poultry seasoning
- 2 cans cream of chicken soup
- 2 cans cream of mushroom soup
- 4.5 oz jar mushrooms, roughly chopped (optional)
- 16 oz chicken broth
- 1 ½ large onions, finely chopped
- 1 large bell pepper, finely chopped
- 4 celery ribs, finely chopped
- 1/2 stick butter
- 4 eggs

Turkey

1. Preheat oven to 325°F (165°C).
2. Pat the outside and inside of the turkey dry with paper towels.
3. Rub the bird with several pats of butter. Combine salt black pepper, onion powder, garlic powder, paprika, and thyme. Sprinkle inside and outside of the turkey. Fold the wing tips under the bird and place the turkey in a roasting pan. Add a bit of butter and seasoning underneath the skin.
4. Place 2 tbsp butter, onions, celery, and bell peppers in the roasting pan.
5. Place turkey, breast side up, on top of the vegetables in the roasting pan.
6. Add giblets to the roaster and 2 cups of water.
7. Bake the turkey, uncovered, in the preheated oven until juices run clear, about 13 minutes per pound, roughly 3 hours. Insert meat thermometer into the thickest part of the thigh; it should read 180°F (82°C). Remove the turkey from the oven and allow it to rest for at least 10 to 15 minutes before slicing. Do not discard the liquid from the bird.

Dressing

1. Remove giblets from the roaster and rough chop giblets. Reserve half of the giblets for the dressing and half for the gravy.
2. In a large mixing bowl, combine cornbread (break up cornbread with your hands in large pieces), half of the cooked chopped giblets, cooked vegetables, black pepper, salt, sage, poultry seasoning, cans of soup, mushrooms, chicken broth, and eggs.
3. Mix all these ingredients together. If more moisture is needed, add juice from the cooked turkey. The mixture should be soupy but not runny.
4. Place the roaster back into the oven and bake for 45 minutes to an hour. The dressing will cook from the outer edges first, moving towards the center of the roaster. When the center of the dressing is firm with no liquid present and holds together, the dressing is done.

Giblet Gravy

1. Giblets cooked and seasoned
2. 1 can cream of mushroom soup
3. 1 can cream of chicken soup
4. 2 boiled eggs
5. Black Pepper (to taste)

- Combine all ingredients for gravy in a medium saucepan and warm over medium heat for approximately 15 minutes.

MAKE IT YOUR OWN

Easy Chicken Enchiladas

INGREDIENTS

- 6-8 c water for boiling
- 1 whole chicken, seasoned, boiled, deboned, and shredded
- ½ Tbsp salt
- ½ Tbsp black pepper
- 1 tsp garlic powder
- 1 tsp onion powder
- 1 can cream of chicken soup
- 1 can cream of mushroom soup
- 1 can chicken broth
- 1 small onion, diced
- 2 Tbsp olive oil
- 1 lb. cheddar cheese, grated
- 1 pkg. corn tortillas

Directions

1. Season chicken with salt, pepper, garlic powder and onion powder.
2. Place in a large, heavy pot, and add water.
3. Cook on medium-high heat for approximately 80-90 minutes or until done.
4. Remove the cooked chicken from the broth. Cool and shred the meat, discarding the bones and skin. Set the meat aside.
5. Preheat oven to 350°F.
6. In a frying pan, sauté onions until translucent. Add the onions to the shredded chicken.

MAKE IT YOUR OWN

Directions

7. In a medium saucepan, combine cream of chicken, cream of mushroom, and broth. Mix well and warm through.

8. In a 13X9 baking dish, ladle enough sauce to cover the bottom.

9. Divide the sauce in half, mixing one-half in with the cooked chicken until well combined.

10. Dip a corn tortilla in the remaining sauce, place the tortilla in the baking dish and add approximately 1 Tbsp of chicken and another of cheddar. Roll the tortilla and place the seam side down.

11. Repeat the previous step until the pan is full. Pour any additional sauce over the enchiladas. Cover with aluminum foil and bake approximately 30 minutes.

12. Remove the pan from the oven and the foil from the pan. Sprinkle the remaining cheese over the enchiladas.

13. Return the pan to the oven and continue cooking until the cheese is melted and begins to brown.

Cook's Tip

- If time is an issue, consider using a rotisserie chicken instead.

Mississippi Pot Roast

INGREDIENTS

- 3-4 lb. Chuck roast
- Salt and pepper to taste
- 2 Tbsp flour to lightly dredge chuck roast
- 2 Tbsp canola oil
- 1 pkg of Hidden Valley Ranch dressing mix
- 1 pkg of Au Jus gravy mix
- ¾ stick of cold butter cut into pieces
- ½ jar of pepperoncini peppers and liquid

MAKE IT YOUR OWN

Directions

1. Preheat the slow cooker to low. In a small mixing bowl, mix each ingredient and the Au Jus gravy mix. Set aside.
2. Rinse and pat dry the chuck roast.
3. Salt and pepper the meat, then lightly dredge flour on all sides of the roast. Shake off excess flour before setting aside.
4. In a cast iron skillet, heat canola oil over medium-high heat until the oil is hot. Add the floured roast and brown on all sides.
5. Sprinkle half of the gravy mixture in the slow cooker, add the roast, then add the other half on top of the roast. Place butter all around the roast. Add peppers and liquid.
6. Place the lid on the slow cooker and cook on low for approximately 7 hours.

Cook's Tip

- It is **not** recommended to cook on high for half the time.

Wade's Classic Sunday Pot Roast

INGREDIENTS

- 1 3-5 lb. chuck, brisket or round roast, at room temperature
- 1 ½ tsp meat tenderizer
- 4 garlic cloves, crushed
- Salt and pepper to taste
- 2 Tbsp flour
- 3 Tbsp canola oil
- ½ c water or beef broth
- 1 small onion, quartered, then cut in half
- ½ lb. of red potatoes, quartered
- ½ lb. carrots, peeled and cut into bite-sized pieces

Directions

1. Preheat oven to 350°F.
2. Remove the roast from the packaging, rinse, and pat dry with paper towels to remove excess water.
3. Season the meat with tenderizer, salt, and pepper.
4. Pierce the beef and insert pieces of garlic. Repeat on all sides until garlic is used.
5. Lightly dust the beef with flour, shaking off any excess.
6. In a large, heavy skillet, add oil and heat on medium-high.
7. Once the pan and oil are hot, add beef and brown on all sides.
8. Place beef in an oven-safe dish with moderate sides. Add liquid and cover with a fitted lid or heavy aluminum foil, sealing the dish well.
9. Cook for approximately 2.5 hours or 40 minutes per pound.
10. Approximately 20 minutes before it is done, remove the cover and add vegetables.
11. Reseal and return to oven to continue cooking for the remaining time.

MiMi's Sure-To-Please Pot Roast

INGREDIENTS

- 1 3-5 lb chuck, brisket, or round roast, at room temperature
- 1 ½ tsp meat tenderizer
- Salt and pepper to taste
- 1 can golden mushroom soup
- 1 envelope of Lipton onion soup mix
- 1 can Sprite or 7UP
- 1 Tbsp flour
- 1 Reynolds Kitchens oven bag

Directions

1. Preheat oven to 350°F.
2. Remove the roast from packaging, rinse, and pat dry with paper towels to remove excess water.
3. Season meat with tenderizer, salt, and pepper.
4. Pour flour into the oven bag and shake to cover; then put floured bag into a 13X9 baking dish.
5. Place the roast into the bag, adding soup and soup mix. Cover all sides. Pour in the soda. Close the bag with the tie provided.
6. Cook for approximately 40 minutes per pound.

Cook's Tip

- Buying a pot roast: The term "pot roast" is not a cut of meat. It is a technique of cooking slowly with a small amount of liquid. Shop for chuck, brisket, round, etc. A tougher cut of meat works best for the long cooking process.
- Boneless vs. Bone-in: When deciding on boneless or bone-in, remember that boneless meats cook faster, but bone-in cuts are more flavorful. You decide.

"Stick to the recipe. Stop all that improvising!" —**Aunt Carolyn**

Gabby's Sweet Chili Glazed Salmon

INGREDIENTS

- 4-6 salmon fillets, approximately ½ lb. each
- ¼ c sweet chili sauce
- 1 ½ Tbsp orange marmalade
- 3 Tbsp soy sauce
- ½ teaspoon ginger purée, optional
- 1 garlic clove, minced
- 2 Tbsp green onions, minced (plus more for garnish)
- Salt and pepper to taste
- Cooking spray

Directions

1. Examine the fish for scales. If present, run a knife opposite the scales to remove.
2. Rinse and pat dry the fillets. Salt and pepper each piece.
3. In a medium mixing bowl, whisk together chili sauce, marmalade, ginger purée, if desired, soy sauce and garlic. Pour into a sealable one-gallon-sized plastic freezer bag, reserving ¼ cup of the mixture for a glaze.
4. Add fish to the bag and place it in the refrigerator for 1 hour.
5. After marinating, remove the fish from the refrigerator to allow the fillets' temperature to rise to room temperature.
6. Adjust the top oven rack to at least 6" from the top of the oven and preheat the oven broiler. In a shallow baking pan, line with aluminum foil and spray with cooking spray.
7. Remove the fish fillets from the marinade and place the pieces skin side down on the prepared pan.
8. Broil for approximately 20 minutes or until browned and flaky in the center.
9. Warm the reserved sauce through and spoon it over the fish. Garnish with green onions.

Serving suggestions: Serve atop saffron rice and grilled asparagus.

White Fish in Cream Sauce (The "Company Fish")

The name says it all! It's called "company fish" because it's what you cook when company comes over. It's simple and elegant, and if you pull it off, it's a restaurant-quality meal. If you want an impressive meal for a fish lover, or someone who wants a lighter meal, this is it.

INGREDIENTS

- 2 lbs orange roughy (or your favorite thick, white fish)
- ½ stick butter (4 Tbsp)
- ¼ c white wine (Chardonnay, Zinfandel, Sauvignon Blanc, etc.)
- 1-pint heavy whipping cream
- Salt and pepper to taste

MAKE IT YOUR OWN

Directions

1. Preheat oven to 350°F.
2. Lightly salt and pepper the fish. Place the fish in a single layer in a shallow baking dish (Stoneware is great. Pyrex is also good).
3. Bake for 10-15 minutes.
4. Remove the dish from the oven.
5. Pour in whipping cream and wine. Cut butter into several pieces and add to the dish.
6. Return the fish to the oven and continue to bake for an additional 15-20 minutes or until the wine/cream sauce is thickened and bubbly.

Cook's Tip

- A beautiful plate of food has lots of variety (i.e., color, texture, etc.)
- Serve the above with saffron rice and asparagus for an easy yet elegant meal.
- Ladle sauce over the fish and rice if desired.

Egg Rolls in a Bowl (Low carb)

Make this when you want to save money on Chinese takeout or when you want dinner on the table in less than 30 minutes.

INGREDIENTS

- 1 lb. ground pork sausage
- 1 ½ tsp toasted sesame oil
- 1 small bag coleslaw mix
- ¼ c carrots, finely shredded
- 4 garlic cloves, minced
- 1 Tbsp minced ginger
- 1 Tbsp soy sauce
- ¼ c green onions
- Sweet and sour sauce or sriracha for serving, optional

Directions

1. Heat a large sauté pan over medium heat, then add sesame oil and sausage. Cook through until done.
2. Add coleslaw, carrots, garlic, ginger, and soy sauce.
3. Cook for approximately 3-5 minutes or until vegetables begin to soften.

When serving, add sweet and sour sauce and/or sriracha if desired.

MAKE IT YOUR OWN

N.O.L.A. Style Red Beans and Rice

INGREDIENTS

- 1 lb. red beans
- 6-8 c water
- 1 lb. Andouille or smoked sausage, sliced
- 1 onion, finely chopped
- 1/2 c celery, chopped
- 1/2 c of bell peppers, chopped
- 3 garlic cloves, minced
- 2 Tbsp butter
- 2 cans chicken broth
- 1 Bay leaf
- Salt and pepper to taste (start with 2 tsp each)
- 2 tsp Cajun seasoning

Directions

1. Rinse and inspect beans, removing any broken beans, pebbles, or dirt.
2. In a large, heavy pot, fry sausage until done, about 5 minutes. Remove sausage, leaving drippings (that's flavor).
3. Add onions, bell pepper, celery, and butter. Cook until onions are nearly translucent. Add garlic.
4. Continue cooking/stirring for another 2-3 minutes.
5. Add broth, water, Bay leaf, and seasonings. On high heat, boil for about 15 minutes. Lower heat, cover, and cook on medium-low for another hour.
6. Remember to check the pot and stir occasionally during cooking.
7. Every range cooks at a different rate; add more water if needed. When beans reach your preferred softness, beans are done. If you would prefer thicker broth, use a fork to mash a few beans in the bottom of the pot and stir.

Serving suggestions

- This may be the original one-dish meal. Serve in a bowl atop a bed of rice or with a slice of your best cornbread.

Gabby's Chicken Fried Rice

INGREDIENTS

- 4 c of day-old rice
- 3 eggs, whisked
- 4 Tbsp toasted sesame oil
- 2 c peas and carrots, frozen
- ½ c scallions, sliced
- 4 Tbsp soy sauce
- 1 c chicken breast or thigh, cubed
- Salt to taste

Directions

1. Salt and pepper chicken breast.
2. In a frying pan, heat 1 Tbsp sesame oil. Sear the chicken and cook through.
3. Once done, allow the chicken to rest.
4. In a saucepan, warm frozen peas and carrots.
5. In a large sauté pan, add rice and warm through.
6. Add oil and create a well in the center of the rice. Add eggs with a dash of salt and pepper and scramble. Mix into rice.
7. Add cooked chicken and peas and carrots.
8. Pour in soy sauce.
9. In the last 3 minutes of cooking, add scallions.

Options

- You may substitute shrimp for chicken or mix the two together for a variation of tastes.

Cook's tip

- Beating vs. whisking eggs. Both techniques are used to combine egg yolks and whites together. Though the terms are often used interchangeably, whisking allows for more air to be incorporated into the eggs, resulting in a lighter texture.

Braised Short Ribs in Dark Beer Sauce

INGREDIENTS

- 2 ½ lbs bone-in beef short ribs
- Salt and pepper to taste
- 1/2 c all-purpose flour
- 2 Tbsp "light tasting" olive oil
- 12oz bottle dark beer like a stout or porter
- 1/4 tsp dried thyme
- 3 garlic cloves, thinly sliced
- 1 medium onion, quartered then sliced
- 1 Tbsp tomato paste
- 1 Tbsp butter
- 2 tsp dark brown sugar
- 2 tsp balsamic vinegar
- Green onions, sliced

Directions

1. Allow the short ribs to rest until at room temperature. Season with salt and pepper, then dust with flour. Set aside.
2. In a medium frying pan, add oil and heat over medium-high heat. Once the oil is hot, add short ribs and brown on all sides.
3. Remove the ribs and place them in a slow cooker set to low.
4. Add thyme, onions, garlic, and beer. Cook on low for 4-5 hours or until meat falls off the bone. If you do not have a slow cooker, place ribs in an oven-safe dish, cover tightly, and cook in the oven on 300°F for approximately 2 ½ -3 hours.

5. Once done, place the ribs on a platter and cover again.

6. Strain the liquid from the slow cooker or pan into a saucepan. Should be approximately 2 cups. Warm through, uncovered, on medium heat.

7. Once the liquid simmers, stir in tomato paste, butter, brown sugar, and vinegar. Lower heat and simmer slowly. Reduce sauce until it thickens, approximately 15 minutes.

8. Once plated for individual serving, ladle sauce over the meat and sprinkle with green onions.

Cook's Recommendation

- Serve with Garlic Cheese Grits and steamed broccoli for an impressive plate.

MAKE IT YOUR OWN

BBQ Kabobs

This recipe is completely changeable and scalable to suit your tastes. Use whatever you have in the fridge. Substitutions are allowed.

INGREDIENTS

- 1 bottle Sweet Vidalia Onion salad dressing
- 2 pkg Barbeque skewers, if wooden, soak in water before use.
- Lawry's seasoning salt

Suggested vegetables:

- Cherry tomatoes
- Mushrooms
- Onions
- Zucchini
- Broccoli
- Cauliflower

Suggested meats:

- Chicken breast or thighs, boneless
- Rib-eye or other tender cuts of beef, cubed
- Earl Campbell's sausage links
- Shrimp, large cleaned

Directions

1. Slice vegetables to equal size.
2. Season the meat with seasoning salt and marinate it in salad dressing.
3. On skewers, alternate meat and vegetables, and grill until meat is done.
4. Remove from the grill, let it rest, and enjoy

MAKE IT YOUR OWN

Italian Stuffed Chicken with an Herb Cream Sauce

CHICKEN

- 4 boneless, skinless chicken breast halves, flattened to about 1 in. thickness
- Salt and pepper to taste
- ½ tsp meat tenderizer
- ½ c. cream cheese, softened (half block)
- ½ c. shredded part-skim mozzarella cheese
- ½ c. chopped fresh spinach (stems removed)
- ½ c. oil-packed sun-dried tomatoes, chopped
- 2 cloves garlic, minced
- ¼ tsp each of seasoned salt and black pepper
- 3 Tbsp butter
- 1 Tbsp olive oil
- Kitchen twine

SAUCE

- ¾ c. chicken broth
- ¼ c. oil-packed sun-dried tomatoes, chopped
- 3 tsps shallots, chopped
- 3 garlic cloves, minced
- 6 fresh basil leaves, thinly sliced
- ¾ c. heavy whipping cream
- ¼ c. butter, cubed

MAKE IT YOUR OWN

Directions

1. With a meat mallet, pound chicken to about 1" thick.
2. Season with salt, pepper, and tenderizer. Set aside.
3. In a small bowl, combine cream cheese, mozzarella, spinach, sun-dried tomatoes, garlic, seasoned salt, and black pepper. Mix well.
4. Spoon the stuffing in the center of the flattened chicken. Roll the chicken around the stuffing, pinwheel style, and secure it with kitchen twine. Do not overfill.
5. Preheat oven to 400°F.
6. In a large frying pan, heat olive oil. Add butter. Brown the chicken on all sides. Transfer the chicken to an ungreased baking dish with sides. Bake uncovered, at 400°F for 20-25 minutes or until juices run clear.
7. Remove the chicken from the oven and let it rest for at least 20 minutes.
8. In a small saucepan, combine broth, tomatoes, shallots, garlic, and basil.
9. Bring to a boil over medium heat. Reduce by half. Add cream and butter. Bring to a boil. Reduce heat; simmer uncovered. Stir often.
10. Slice the rolls diagonally and place them on dinner plates to serve.
11. Serve the sauce alongside the chicken. Avoid ladling over chicken, as diners should decide whether to add.

Cook's Tip

- Start browning the rollup near its seam.
- In the kitchen, a sharp knife is a safer knife.
- If you do not have access to a meat thermometer, a good rule of thumb is that the chicken is done when the juices run clear.

Serving Suggestions

- Serve atop saffron rice and herbed broccoli

MAKE IT YOUR OWN

Quesadillas - Bean and Cheese

INGREDIENTS

- 2 Tbsp butter
- 2 flour tortillas
- 1/4 c refried beans
- 1/4 c Colby jack cheese
- 2 Tbsp water
- 1 1/2 tsp olive oil
- Salt and pepper to taste

Directions

1. Place refried beans into a small saucepan. Add water, olive oil, and stir until well mixed. Taste and add salt and pepper.
2. On a griddle or in two large frying pans, heat on medium-high, add 1 Tbsp butter, and spread it across the pan/griddle. Place both tortillas on the buttered surface and allow to brown on both sides.
3. Remove tortillas and spread toasted side with refried beans.
4. Add the last Tbsp of butter to the griddle or pans. Place the untoasted side of the tortillas in a pan.
5. Sprinkle with cheese and allow the cheese to melt slightly. Fold one tortilla on top of the other so that beans and cheese meet. With a spatula, press the quesadilla together. Flip the quesadilla and lightly press again.
6. Remove the quesadilla from the pan and cut it into 4-8 pieces. Best served immediately.

Serving Suggestions

- Quesadillas are a fun, quick, and portable meal. Serve with your favorite topping, including salsa, sour cream, or avocados.

MAKE IT YOUR OWN

Quesadillas - Spinach and Mushrooms

INGREDIENTS

- 3 Tbsp olive oil
- 1/2 c onions, finely chopped
- 2 garlic cloves, minced
- 4 c fresh spinach, washed and patted dry
- Salt and pepper to taste
- 1/4 c Colby jack cheese
- 2 Tbsp butter
- 2 flour tortillas

Directions

1. In a large sauté pan, heat 2 Tbsp oil over medium-high heat. Add onions and sauté until nearly translucent. In the last 2-4 minutes of cooking, add garlic, spinach, 1 tsp salt, and 1/4 tsp of pepper to onions and keep stirring until done. Remove the mixture from the pan.
2. On a griddle or in two large frying pans, heat on medium-high; add 1 Tbsp of butter and spread the butter across the pan/griddle. Place both tortillas on the buttered pan or griddle surface and allow to brown.
3. Remove the tortillas.
4. Add 1 Tbsp of butter to the griddle or pans. Place the untoasted side of the tortillas in the pan and spread the browned side with the cheese and spinach mixture.
5. Flip one tortilla on top of the other so that spinach and cheese are inside. With a spatula, press the quesadilla together. Flip the quesadilla and lightly press again.
6. Remove the quesadillas from the pan and cut them into 4-8 pieces. Best if served immediately.

MAKE IT YOUR OWN

_____
_____
_____
_____
_____

Mediterranean Baked Chicken

INGREDIENTS

- 1 c fresh lemon juice,
- 4 Tbsp of lemon zest
- 10 large cloves of garlic, minced,
- 1 1/4 c extra virgin olive oil
- 1 1/2 Tbsp dried oregano,
- 1 tsp red chili flakes
- 2 tsp salt
- 1 tsp black pepper
- 1 lb boneless chicken breast or thighs

Directions

1. In a gallon-sized sealable plastic bag, combine all of the ingredients, except the chicken, and seal.
2. Rinse and pat dry the chicken, then place it into the marinade. Ensure all sides are covered.
3. Place the bag in the refrigerator for up to 18 hours.
4. Preheat oven to 400°F. Remove the chicken from the marinade and add it to a baking dish with sides.
5. Make sure the dish is large enough for the pieces of chicken not to touch one another.
6. Pour the remaining marinade over the chicken.
7. Bake uncovered for 60-90 minutes or until chicken is done.

MAKE IT YOUR OWN

Quick Meatloaf

INGREDIENTS

- 2 lbs. ground beef
- 2 eggs, beaten
- 1/4 c toasted breadcrumbs
- 1/2 c milk
- 1/2 c chili sauce
- 1/2 pkg meatloaf seasoning
- 2 Tbsp your favorite steak sauce
- 1 Tbsp mayonnaise

Directions

1. Preheat oven to 375°F.
2. In a large mixing bowl, combine ground beef, eggs, breadcrumbs, milk, 2 Tbsp chili sauce, seasoning, steak sauce, and mayonnaise. Mix well but be sure not to overwork.
3. Form a loaf with the meat mixture. Place it in a 13 x 9 baking dish and bake for approximately 50 minutes.
4. Spread the remaining chili sauce on top of the meatloaf and bake for an additional 10 minutes or until done.

Cook's Tip

1. Re: Beef —80-20 beef is best for flavor. 90-10 has less fat.
2. Do not overwork the mixture, or the meatloaf will become dense.

MAKE IT YOUR OWN

Classic Sunday Meatloaf

INGREDIENTS

- 2 c yellow onion, finely chopped
- 2 Tbsp olive oil
- 1 tsp fresh thyme
- 1 tsp oregano
- 2 garlic cloves, minced
- 2 1/2 lb. ground beef
- 2 tsp dry steak seasoning
- 1 tsp black pepper
- 3 Tbsp Worcestershire sauce
- 1/3 c chicken broth
- 2 Tbsp mayonnaise
- 1 c plus 2 Tbsp chili sauce
- 2 slices of toasted bread, crushed
- 2 large eggs

Directions

1. Preheat oven to 325°F.
2. In a large sauté pan, heat olive oil over medium heat. Add onions, thyme, oregano, steak seasoning, black pepper, and cook over medium heat until translucent. Add garlic and cook another 2-4 minutes. Lower heat, then add Worcestershire sauce, chicken stock, and 2 Tbsp chili sauce. Combine, remove from heat, and allow to cool.
3. In a large bowl, combine beef, onion mixture, eggs, mayonnaise, and breadcrumbs. Mix well, but do not overwork.
4. Form a loaf with the meat mixture. Place it in a 13 x 9 baking dish with sides and bake for approximately 1hr.
5. Spread the remaining chili sauce on top of the meatloaf and bake for an additional 10 minutes or until done.

MAKE IT YOUR OWN

Homemade Pizza

INGREDIENTS

- 1 prepackaged pizza crust
- ½ c pizza sauce
- ¾ c Italian sausage
- 10-12 turkey pepperoni slices
- 1 c mozzarella cheese, shredded
- ¼ c Parmesan cheese
- 4 mozzarella pearls
- ¼ onion, thinly sliced
- ¾ bell pepper, thinly sliced
- Sliced mushrooms, optional

Directions

1. Preheat oven to 400°F.
2. In a sauté pan, crumble, brown, and drain the Italian sausage. Set aside.
3. In the pan used for sausage, sauté onions and peppers until onions are nearly translucent.
4. Place pizza crust on a foil-lined baking sheet or pizza pan.
5. Ladle pizza sauce onto the crust and distribute evenly.
6. Sprinkle half of the shredded mozzarella over the entire pizza.
7. Add all other ingredients.
8. Add the remaining cheese.
9. Bake for 15-20 minutes or until desired doneness.

MAKE IT YOUR OWN

Hot Italian Sausage and Pasta

This is not your ordinary spaghetti dinner; serve it when you'd like a comforting meal but not the usual fare. It's quick, serves a crowd, and is a delicious leftover.

INGREDIENTS

- 1 lb hot Italian sausage
- 1 Tbsp butter
- 1 lb Cavatappi pasta
- 2 Tbsp garlic, minced
- ½ onion, diced
- ¼ c sun-dried tomatoes, diced
- 2 Tbsp tomato paste
- 6-8oz fresh spinach
- 1 c white wine
- 1 ¼ c heavy whipping cream
- 2 Tbsp crème fraiche
- 1 c Parmesan, fresh
- 1 c mozzarella
- Seasoning salt and black pepper to taste
- ¼ tsp crushed red pepper flakes
- Parsley

Directions

1. In a large saucepan, add salt, and butter to boiling water and cook the pasta until just done. Do not overcook. Remove from heat, drain pasta, rinse in cool water, and continue to drain. Set aside.

2. In a large frying pan, over medium-high heat, cook the Italian sausage until it's nearly done. Add onion, continuing to stir to avoid scorching. Stir in garlic, sundried tomatoes, and tomato paste. Toss in spinach, seasoning salt, black pepper, and red pepper flakes.

3. Add white wine to deglaze the pan by stirring up the bits on the bottom of the pan. Reduce heat to medium. Pour in heavy whipping cream and continue to stir, then bring to a simmer.

4. Stir in crème fraiche, Parmesan cheese, and mozzarella. Add the pasta and stir to combine.

5. Plate the pasta and garnish with more Parmesan cheese and a sprinkle of parsley, if desired.

Annie's Perfectly Fried Chicken

Great fried chicken begins with making plenty of decisions. Here are some:

- First, size matters! Select smaller birds known as fryers — the larger the pieces, the more difficult they are to fry well.
- Next, you CANNOT rush the preparation time. Period! Forced thawing (by submerging or by holding the chicken under running water) usually results in an unattractive, bloody-looking interior, especially near the bone. Remember, water is the natural enemy of fried foods.
- Also, to achieve the maximum flavor, season both the chicken and the flour.
- The selection of your fry vessel is also important. A cast iron skillet is recommended. However, using a large, heavy pot will be helpful if you are just learning or have lots of chicken to fry.
- Be careful to keep the oil at a consistent temperature. Do not overcrowd your pan.
- A lid is important, though many experts reject this method.
- Lastly, the key to perfectly fried chicken is to recognize that hearing is just as important as sight to the end result. When the sound of frying starts to become quiet, the chicken is ready.

MAKE IT YOUR OWN

INGREDIENTS	MAKE IT YOUR OWN

- 15-20oz cooking oil, depending on size of frying vessel
- 2 lbs chicken fryer pieces, thawed and cut into parts
- 2 c all-purpose flour in a large, sealable storage bag
- 1 Tbsp soy sauce
- ½ Tbsp salt
- ½ Tbsp black pepper
- 1 tsp Lawry's seasoned salt
- 1 tsp garlic powder
- 1 tsp onion powder
- 1 tsp paprika

Directions

1. In a deep fat fryer, fill with oil 2/3 of the way and preheat to 375°F.
2. Remove the chicken from its packaging and rinse it under cold water. Pat the chicken dry to remove any excess water. Lay the chicken in a large dish. Add soy sauce and toss until all pieces are well coated.
3. In a small bowl, add salt, black pepper, seasoned salt, onion powder, garlic powder, and paprika. Whisk together until well combined.
4. Sprinkle enough of the dry ingredients to thoroughly coat the chicken. Allow the chicken to marinate for at least 30 minutes, being sure to keep the chicken at a safe temperature.
5. Add the remaining seasoning to the bag of flour and shake until the seasonings are well distributed throughout the flour.

6. Place the marinated chicken into the bag of seasoned flour, a few pieces at a time. Seal the bag, coat the chicken pieces, remove the chicken, and shake off excess flour. Repeat until all pieces are dredged.

7. Before frying, test the oil to ensure it is hot. If you do not have a thermometer, look to see if the heated oil is moving, then place a pinch of flour into the hot oil. If the flour remains together or sinks, the oil isn't hot enough. If the flour seems to fry and move rapidly, it's ready.

8. GENTLY place the chicken into the fryer. Fill the fryer, but do not overfill as this will cause the oil's temperature to drop. Pay close attention to the sound the chicken makes as it enters the vessel. Observe the chicken for 1-2 minutes to ensure the oil won't overflow while cooking. Place the lid on and allow to fry in approximately 5–10-minute intervals before carefully removing the lid and checking the progress.

9. Look for a brown outline around each piece. Once spotted, lift the piece, examine the bottom for a golden-brown color, and turn to cook the other side. Each piece of chicken will fry at a slightly different rate, so treat each piece individually. Once both sides are golden brown and the oil starts to become quiet, remove each piece.

10. If cooking a large amount of chicken, be prepared to add additional oil to the vessel.

JACQUI'S DAUGHTER, INGRID, ON RIGHT. HER MOM, MY SISTER, WAS THE INSPIRATION FOR THIS RECIPE

Aunt Jacqui's Salmon Croquettes

If you got the chance to meet Jacqueline, you would know she was faith, goodness, and intelligence in human form. My sister didn't say a lot; she let results and her living say it all. Everything she touched was left better — including her family and their cooking skills. Jacqui finished her race and went to collect her crown in Heaven. I'm sure you are wondering what this has to do with cooking. Well, anything built rests on a foundation. Jacqui was our culinary foundation. Part historian, part innovator, she could build communities, families, and futures with the simplest things, all from her kitchen.

INGREDIENTS

- 1 can pink salmon, drained
- ½ medium onion, finely chopped
- The green tops of 1 scallion, finely sliced
- ¼ c cornmeal
- 2 Tbsp all-purpose flour
- 2 eggs, beaten
- Salt and pepper to taste
- ¼ tsp Old Bay seasoning
- ¼ c canola or your favorite cooking oil

Directions

1. In a large mixing bowl, add the first eight ingredients. Mix well until thoroughly combined. Form croquettes in 2-3" disks. Set aside.
2. Preheat a cast-iron skillet over medium-high heat and add approximately 2 Tbsp of oil. Coat the bottom.
3. Add croquettes but be careful not to crowd the pan. Look for signs of browning on the bottom and flip to cook the other side. Approximately 4 minutes per side. Allow the croquettes to rest. Serve with rice or biscuits.

VEGETABLES AND SIDES

KABOB VEGGIES

A LOVE LETTER

My Love,

If this cookbook were a song, this section is where you'd vamp! These recipes are tradition; however, tradition changes with each new member of the family – blood and otherwise. Vegetables are perfectly approachable and a great place to start improving on the legacy. Use what you've learned. Historically, our diets were rich in nutrition coming straight from the soil. Yet the preparation was all about survival and may not have been the healthiest.

Baby, this is your time to start making your mark on tradition. Improve what you find here. Remember, the name of the game has always been to do better than the ones who came before you, even in feeding and loving each other. And truth be told, we're excited to learn a better way from you.

AJ's Sautéed Spinach (Vegetarian)

This is a quick side dish, taking approximately 20 minutes from start to finish. The longer you cook spinach, the smaller the yield. Your 8 cups of greens can be reduced to 1-2 cups.

INGREDIENTS

- 1 bag of spinach, or approximately 8 cups
- 3 Tbsp "light tasting" olive oil
- ½ medium onion, diced
- 4 garlic cloves, minced
- 2-3 Tbsp butter
- Salt and pepper to taste

MAKE IT YOUR OWN

Directions

1. Rinse and drain the spinach (water removal is important).
2. In a frying or sauté pan, heat the oil on medium and add the onion to sauté.
3. Just before the onions are fully translucent, add garlic and continue cooking for another 2-3 minutes.
4. Increase heat to medium-high and add spinach leaves.
5. Add salt and pepper and stir continuously until leaves wilt.
6. Keep stirring and add the butter to finish.

Cook's Tip

- Some foods have a natural affinity for one another. Spinach and chicken, in any cuisine, is an excellent pairing.

Uncle Jay's Scalloped Potatoes

INGREDIENTS

- 6 medium russet potatoes, peeled and sliced into 1/4" disks
- 3 Tbsp unsalted butter cut into 1/4" pats
- Salt to taste
- Pepper to taste
- 1 ½ tsp garlic powder
- 1 tsp onion powder
- 1 qt Heavy whipping cream (more or less depending on the pan)
- 8 oz Cracker Barrel extra sharp yellow block, shredded and divided

Directions

1. Preheat oven to 350°F.
2. Under cool, running water, rinse the potatoes to rub away any dirt or debris.
3. Peel the potatoes and cut them into 1/2" disks. Place the potatoes in a shallow, oven-safe dish in a single layer with a small overlap.
4. Add butter throughout
5. Sprinkle evenly with salt, pepper, garlic powder, and onion powder.
6. Cover the potatoes with heavy whipping cream and place them in the oven uncovered and allow to cook until softened (approximately 45 minutes).
7. Once softened, add the cheese and continue to bake until the cheese melts and the cream thickens and begins to bubble (approximately 20 minutes).
8. Remove from the oven and allow it to cool before serving. Potatoes will be extremely hot.

"Just try it. Don't be scared."
—Lady B

Mango-Brown Sugar Glazed Sweet Potatoes

INGREDIENTS

- 2 medium sweet potatoes
- 3 Tbsp butter cut in pieces (plus extra to butter pan)
- ½ tsp salt
- 2 Tbsp brown sugar
- ½ tsp butter flavoring
- ½ c fresh mango juice (usually in the refrigerated produce section)

Directions

1. Scrub whole potatoes and place them in a medium saucepan, then cover them with water and half of the mango juice.
2. Parboil the potatoes so that the potatoes soften but do not cook through.
3. Preheat the oven to 350°F and butter the bottom of the baking dish just as you would a cake pan.
4. Remove the potatoes from the heat, remove the potatoes from the saucepan, and allow them to cool to the touch. Discard water.
5. Peel the outer skin from the potatoes, then cut them into ½" thick disks.
6. Spread the potatoes in a single layer with a slight overlap between each disk.
7. Top with butter, salt, and brown sugar.
8. Mix flavoring and mango juice, then drizzle the mixture over the potatoes.
9. Bake until done, approximately 40 minutes or until tender.

MAKE IT YOUR OWN

Friend's Shaved Cajun Brussels Sprouts (Vegan)

The "auntie" who introduced me to this recipe is a dear old friend. She had a much more thoughtful approach to food than me, Ms. "Go-Big-Or-Go-Home." In her approach, you can actually appreciate the food more when it is at its simplest. Families matter, but so do great friendships.

INGREDIENTS

- 12-16oz fresh Brussels sprouts
- 2 Tbsp extra virgin (light tasting) olive oil
- ½ Tbsp Tony Chachere's Original Creole Seasoning
- Pepper sauce, to taste, optional

Directions

1. Remove the outer leaves and examine the sprouts for dirt, insects, sand, etc.
2. Slice sprouts into thin ribbons, discarding the stem and fibrous core. Wash sprouts and dry excess water.
3. In a sauté pan, heat oil at medium-high and add vegetables, stirring constantly.
4. Add creole seasoning and continue cooking until done, approximately 15 minutes. Do not overcook.

MAKE IT YOUR OWN

_____
_____
_____
_____
_____
_____
_____
_____
_____
_____
_____
_____
_____
_____
_____
_____

Roasted Brussel Sprouts with Bacon

INGREDIENTS

- 1 lb. fresh Brussels Sprouts
- 3 strips of thick-cut bacon
- 4 garlic cloves
- ¼ c onion, chopped
- 2 Tbsp olive oil
- Salt and pepper to taste

MAKE IT YOUR OWN

Directions

1. Preheat oven to 350°F.
2. Remove the outer leaves and examine the sprouts for dirt, insects, sand, etc.
3. Quarter the sprouts and rinse. Spin or pat dry.
4. Cut the sprouts in half along the core.
5. Cook the bacon in a frying pan until done. Drain on a paper towel and set aside.
6. In a baking dish, add olive oil, sprouts, garlic, onions, salt and pepper.
7. Place in the oven and cook to desired tenderness, approximately 20 minutes.
8. Once done, crumble the bacon and toss it in with the sprouts.

Kidney Beans

INGREDIENTS

- 1 lb. red kidney beans
- 1 ham hock or 1 smoked turkey wing
- 1 can chicken or vegetable broth
- 5 c water
- 2 Tbsp butter
- 1/2 c onion, chopped
- 1/4 c celery, chopped
- 4 garlic cloves, roughly chopped
- 1 Bay leaf
- 2 tsp Salt (or to taste)
- 2 tsp pepper (or to taste)
- 1 tsp garlic powder
- 1 tsp Cajun Seasoning
- ½ c ground beef, browned and drained
- 6 c white rice, cooked

Directions

1. Rinse and place the beans in a bowl. Fill the bowl with water, completely submerging the beans.
2. Inspect and discard damaged beans, pebbles, or beans that float. Soak overnight.
3. The next day, in a large, heavy pot, add hock or wing, broth, and water.
4. Cover and cook on medium until the meat pulls away from the bone, approximately 90 minutes.
5. In a sauté pan, melt the butter and sauté the onions to soften, then add celery and cook until nearly translucent. Add garlic and continue cooking for another 2-3 minutes. Add the aromatics and the onion mixture to the pot with the meat.
6. In the same sauté pan (do not wash or wipe out the pan—that is your flavor), brown the ground beef, seasoning with a small amount of salt and pepper.
7. Drain the beef and set it aside. Add bay leaf and other seasonings to pot and cook over low heat for approximately 60 minutes or until tender.
8. If a thicker consistency is desired, mash a few beans in the bottom of the pot with a fork, then stir. Add ground beef and continue cooking for another 30 minutes.
9. Serve in a bowl over cooked rice.

Roasted Zucchini and Summer Squash Mix

INGREDIENTS

- 1/2 lb. zucchini
- 1/2 lb. yellow summer squash
- 1/2 c onions, finely chopped
- 4 cloves garlic, minced
- Salt and pepper to taste
- 1 tsp garlic powder
- 1/8 c extra virgin olive oil
- 1/2 tsp red pepper flakes, optional
- PAM Cooking Spray

MAKE IT YOUR OWN

Directions

1. Preheat oven to 350°F. On a large sheet pan, spray some cooking spray.
2. Rinse zucchini and summer squash under cool running water. Cut vegetables lengthwise in uniform pieces approximately 1/2" in thickness.
3. Add the final ingredients to the pan. Toss by hand until everything is coated with oil and the vegetables are evenly mixed.

Arrange squash mixture in a single layer and roast uncovered until vegetables are soft, approximately 25 minutes. Do not overcook.

White Beans with Pancetta

Ingredients

- 1 lb hot Italian sausage with fennel
- 5 oz pancetta, diced
- 1 yellow onion, diced
- 1 green bell pepper, diced
- 6 cloves garlic, diced
- 1 Tbsp oregano, chopped
- 2 tsp crushed red pepper flakes
- Salt to taste
- Black pepper to taste
- 2 qt chicken stock
- 2 c dried Italian white beans (do not soak)
- 2-3 Tbsp vegetable oil
- 1 Tbsp olive oil
- Fresh green onions
- 1 leek, fried
- Sour cream

Directions

1. In a large stock pot, over medium-high heat, spread the vegetable oil and sear the Italian sausage until brown on all sides; reduce heat to medium and cook until done. Drain oil and set sausage aside.

2. In the same pan, add the olive oil and sauté the pancetta until crisp, add the onions and cook until they take on color, add the garlic and cook an additional 2–3 minutes until lightly toasted.

3. Add the remaining ingredients, except the sausage, bring to a rapid boil, then simmer for approximately two hours until the beans begin to cream. Reduce to a simmer.

4. Dice the sausage and add it back to the pot. You will likely need to add some additional water or stock as it reduces. If a thicker consistency is desired, use a fork and mash a few beans in the bottom of the pot. Stir to thicken.

5. Cut the white part of the leeks into matchstick-sized pieces. Place in boiling water for 15 seconds, squeeze dry in a paper towel and then fry in a small amount of canola oil until golden. Drain on a paper towel and season with salt and pepper.

6. Serve the beans in a bowl and top with fried leeks, sliced green onions, and a dollop of sour cream.

MAKE IT YOUR OWN

Garlic Cheese Grits

INGREDIENTS

- 2 1/2 c water
- 1/2 tsp salt
- 1 c grits
- 2 Tbsp butter
- ½ c half and half, (+/-) depending on desired thickness
- ½ c grated sharp cheddar cheese
- 2 tsp garlic, minced

Directions

1. Bring water to a boil in a heavy, medium saucepan. Add salt.
2. In a sauté pan, add 1 Tbsp of butter and heat on medium-high heat. Add garlic and cook until slightly translucent. Remove from heat immediately.
3. Whisk grits into boiling water then reduce heat to low. Place the lid on and cook for approximately 25-30 minutes or until grits start to soften. Stir often to avoid scorching and clumping. Add additional liquid if needed. Taste and add more salt if needed.
4. Remove the cover and whisk in the sautéed garlic, cheese, and half and half. Whisk until cheese is melted.
5. Serve while hot.

Cook's tip

- Grits are inedible without enough salt!!

MAKE IT YOUR OWN

Aunt Balenca's Collard Green Hack

This is a great recipe to use when you want big, bold, flavors but don't have time for all the chopping and dicing.

INGREDIENTS

- ½ -1 lb. smoked turkey legs, rinsed
- 2 bunches of Collard greens, destemmed
- 1 can Ro-tel Chunky Diced Tomatoes and Green Chilies

Directions

1. Place collards in a sink. Fill the sink with water and sprinkle with a Tbsp of salt. Agitate the greens. The salty water will act as an abrasive agent cleaning the greens and removing all dirt and possible insects. Repeat several times until the bottom of the sink feels free of grit and sand.
2. Put smoked turkey legs in a slow cooker on low.
3. Drain and stack several leaves together, roll tightly and cut down the middle and then horizontally.
4. Place greens in a slow cooker and cook on low.
5. Check and stir the greens often.
6. When greens are almost done (to taste), add the can of Ro-tel Chunky Diced Tomatoes and Green Chilies and continue cooking until done, then enjoy.

Cook's tip

- No seasoning was needed since the smoked turkey legs and the Ro-tel were used.

MAKE IT YOUR OWN

_____
_____
_____
_____

Sautéed Mushrooms

INGREDIENTS

- ½ lb your favorite mushrooms
- ½ lb portabella mushrooms
- 1 large onion, chopped
- 3 Tbsp butter or oil
- 3 garlic cloves, minced
- 3 Tbsp Madeira wine
- Salt and pepper to taste

MAKE IT YOUR OWN

_____
_____
_____
_____
_____
_____
_____
_____

Directions

1. In a large sauté pan, warm butter or oil until hot but not burned.
2. Add the mushrooms and onions, then sauté them for approximately 10 minutes. Add garlic and cook for an additional 2 minutes. Finish by adding Madeira wine, salt, and pepper. Sauté for another 5 minutes or to desired tenderness.

Serving suggestion

- Serve alongside beef or chicken to add a rich earthiness to your meal.

Term

- **Sauté** – To fry quickly in a small amount of fat. This technique is ideal for cooking small pieces of meat or vegetables.

Turnip Greens

The following recipe will work for most types of greens, including collards and kale. However, please refer to AJ's Sauteed Spinach recipe when cooking spinach.

INGREDIENTS

- 1 Bunch of greens
- 1-4 pieces Seasoning meats (ham hocks, ham bones, smoked turkey necks, smoked turkey wings, etc.)
- 2 boxes Vegetable broth
- 1 Tbsp Ac'cent Flavor Enhancer
- Salt to taste

Directions

1. Examine, pick, cut way tough stems, and cut leaves into 1-2" ribbons. Wash the greens.
2. In a large pot, add seasoning meat and enough vegetable broth to cover the meat throughout cooking time. Cook over medium heat for approximately 2 hours or until the meat falls off the bone. Water can be added if more liquid is needed.
3. During the first wash, add about 1 Tbsp of salt to a sink of cool water and allow the greens to soak in water a few minutes. This will kill any insects that may have been missed while picking greens. Wash greens in a double sink until no grit is left behind in the sink. (After about six washings, your greens should be clean.) Always run your hand along the bottom of the sink to check for sand and grit.
4. Remove the seasoning meat from the pot and debone. (This step is optional).
5. Return the seasoning meat to the pot, then add greens, salt, and Ac'cent.
6. Simmer until the greens are tender (This will take approximately 1 hour).
7. Taste the greens for tenderness.

Cook's tip

- Picking vs washing. Preparing greens (collards, turnips, kale, etc.) for cooking is a two-step process: the first is picking, and the second is washing. Picking is to inspect each leaf, removing any stones, insects, damaged leaves, etc. you can see. Washing is to submerge leaves in cool water, agitating vigorously to remove the dirt and grit you cannot see. Salt may be used in washing to help loosen debris from leaves. Greens should be washed repeatedly until the bottom of the sink or bowl feels clean and free from grit.

- Greens bought in bags are pre-washed and picked. However, always wash greens, though picking bagged greens may not be necessary.

MAKE IT YOUR OWN

Carolyn's Southern Potato Salad

INGREDIENTS

- 5 large Idaho potatoes
- 2 boiled eggs
- ¾ c celery, finely chopped
- ½ c onion, finely chopped
- ½ c sweet pickle salad cubes
- ½ c mayonnaise
- ½ tsp mustard
- 1 tsp sugar
- 1 tsp vinegar
- ½ small jar pimentos
- Salt and pepper to taste
- Dash of paprika, to garnish

Directions

1. Wash, peel, and cube the potatoes.
2. Boil the potatoes in salted water until fork tender.
3. Remove from heat, then drain and rinse with cool water to bring down the temperature and stop the cooking process.
4. Drain the potatoes, place them in a bowl, and refrigerate until cool.
5. Dice boiled eggs and set aside.
6. In a large bowl, mix all ingredients well, except the potatoes.
7. Add potatoes to the mixture and fold until well coated.
8. Refrigerate until ready to serve.

MAKE IT YOUR OWN

DESSERTS

CHOCOLATE CAKE

A LOVE LETTER

My Love,

Never sell yourself short. Whatever talent you have, nurture it! There is a proverb that says, "Your gifts will make room for you." Your smallest skill can provide a sense of self and distinction. Aunt Annie was a great cook and an even better baker. What I remember most from our visits in summer was her routine. She'd get off the bus in her maid's uniform, walk home, and come alive. Annie would turn on the music, pour a glass of her favorite bourbon, and lose herself in the kitchen. Remember, cooking as a means of feeding souls started long before my generation. It was done in the generation before that and the generation before that as long as there has been family. Many times, a good meal is how people got through, how they celebrated, consoled, encouraged, and found courage. It's where they found pride in who they were.

Perhaps they had no chance of becoming CEO, but maybe they could cook everyone else under the table. The aunties and uncles before you had their share of struggles, but they also had their share of joy. Plus, they had something money and society could never give them. They had purpose, faith, and each other.

I suppose a large part of writing all this down is to honor every "Annie" who never received recognition for their genius and not just in the kitchen. They made extraordinary contributions, building families and communities one meal at a time. And you will, too!

Pearl's Peach Cobbler

Mom passed this recipe to me in November 1984. I thought my careful notetaking would yield the same results as she got when making it. Not so! The recipe itself is a teacher and it taught me many lessons. I learned the following: Improvisation is fine for cooking, but baking is pure science! Temperatures matter — for ingredients, the room, and even the work surface. Be precise with your measurements. And practice makes perfect.

FILLING

- 2 large cans sliced peaches, undrained
- ¾ c sugar
- ½ stick butter
- 1 tsp cinnamon
- ½ tsp allspice

CRUST AND DUMPLINGS

- 2 ½ c all-purpose flour
- ½ tsp salt
- ½ c iced water, plus a bit more if needed
- 1 c cold butter, cut into 1/2-inch pieces

Directions

1. In a large bowl, whisk together the flour and salt. Add butter to the flour, coating each piece. With a pastry cutter or your hands, cut the butter into the flour. Continue blending the two until the butter pieces are the size of almonds. (Note: the larger the butter, the flakier the crust. The smaller the pieces, the more unyielding the crust.

2. Create a well in the center of the flour mixture. Add 1/4 cup of ice water and mix together gently to incorporate. Be careful not to overwork the dough. Gradually add water 1 tablespoon at a time and continue incorporating until it becomes a dough. Make sure your dough isn't wet or sticky to the touch.

3. Place dough on plastic wrap, form a disk, wrap tightly, and refrigerate for at least 30 minutes.

4. While dough is chilling, add peaches with liquid, butter, cinnamon, and allspice to a heavy pot, stir gently, and bring to a boil over medium heat. Reduce heat to simmer about 30 minutes or until the filling thickens.

5. Take half the dough from the disk, rewrap the rest, and return to the refrigerator. On a cool surface, dust the surface and rolling pin with flour. Roll the dough to 1/4–inch thickness, cut into 2-inch strips, then cut again into manageable pieces. Add the strips to the simmering peach filling, one piece at a time.

6. Add the desired amount of dough, which will become dumplings, to the filling and cook until well incorporated. Simmer for 10 minutes and reduce heat. Spray cooking spray in a 9X13 baking dish, then add the filling.

7. Preheat oven to 350°F. Unwrap the refrigerated dough, flour a cool surface as well as a rolling pin. Roll out dough to 1/8 – 1/4 inch thickness and place it onto the filling.

8. Press lightly in place, trim the excess, pierce 4-5 times to vent, and bake for 30-40 minutes or until the crust is golden brown. Remove the cobbler from the oven and brush the crust with melted butter. Lightly sprinkle with sugar and cinnamon.

MAKE IT YOUR OWN

Sour Cream Pound Cake

INGREDIENTS

- 1 Duncan Hines Yellow cake mix, butter recipe
- 4 eggs, at room temperature
- ¼ c sugar
- ½ c canola oil
- ¼ c water
- ½ pint sour cream

MAKE IT YOUR OWN

_____
_____
_____
_____
_____
_____
_____
_____

Directions

1. Preheat oven to 375°F. Grease and flour a tube or Bundt pan. Set aside.
2. In a large bowl, mix the cake mix and eggs.
3. Add the sugar, oil, and water.
4. Beat until smooth.
5. Fold in the sour cream.
6. Pour the mixture into a prepared pan and bake for 45 minutes.
7. Let cool, then place on a serving plate.

Lemon Poppy Seed Pound Cake

INGREDIENTS

- 3 c cake flour
- 2 c sugar
- ¼ c poppy seeds
- 1 c butter, softened
- 1 c buttermilk
- 4 eggs, at room temperature
- ½ tsp baking soda
- ½ tsp baking powder
- ½ tsp salt
- 4 tsp grated lemon peel
- ½ tsp butter flavoring
- ½ tsp good vanilla

Icing:

- 1 c powdered sugar
- 1-2 tbsp lemon juice

Directions

1. Heat oven to 325°F.
2. Grease and flour a Bundt or tube pan.
3. In a large mixing bowl, combine all the cake ingredients and beat at low speed, scraping the sides often. Once all ingredients are thoroughly combined, mix on high for an additional 1-2 minutes.
4. Pour the batter evenly into the prepared pan.
5. Bake for approximately 60 minutes until an inserted wooden toothpick comes out clean.
6. Remove from the oven and let cool for 10 minutes.
7. Place a serving plate upside down atop the pan, then flip both over and remove the pan.

8. In a small bowl, combine powdered sugar and lemon juice.
9. Stir until smooth and free of lumps.
10. Drizzle over the cake.

Cook's Tip

- A great batter makes a great cake.
- Allow eggs to come up to room temperature before adding.
- Avoid overbeating!! Overbeating removes air from the batter needed to make cakes light. Cake batter that is overbeaten makes for a dense or "packy" cake.

MAKE IT YOUR OWN

_____
_____
_____
_____
_____
_____
_____
_____
_____
_____
_____
_____

Toni's Magic Margarita Cheesecake

INGREDIENTS

- ¾ c graham crackers, finely crushed
- ½ c salted pretzels, finely crushed
- 10 Tbsp melted butter
- ½ tsp butter flavoring
- ¼ c sugar
- 1 14oz can Eagle Brand Sweetened Condensed milk (NOT evaporated milk!!)
- ⅓ c ReaLime Juice from concentrate
- 3-5 Tbsp tequila
- 2-4 Tbsp triple sec or another orange-flavored liqueur
- 1 c whipped cream

Directions

1. Combine 1st five ingredients. Mix well.
2. Press the mix firmly on the bottom and sides of the lightly buttered baking dish, pie plate, or mold.
3. In a large bowl, combine condensed milk, ReaLime juice, tequila, and triple sec. Mix well.
4. Fold in the whipped cream until fully incorporated but do not overwork.
5. Pour the filling into the crust.
6. Freeze or chill until firm – approximately 4 hours. in the fridge or 2 hours. in the freezer.

MAKE IT YOUR OWN

_____
_____
_____
_____
_____
_____
_____
_____
_____
_____
_____
_____

Auntie Nette's Orange Pound Cake

INGREDIENTS

- 2-1/2 c cake flour plus a bit extra to dust the pan
- 2 c sugar
- 1-1/2 tsp baking powder
- 1/2 tsp baking soda
- 6oz. (12 Tbsp) unsalted butter softened; more for the pan
- 3/4 c canola or other mild-flavored oil (check for freshness before using)
- 1-1/2 Tbsp finely minced lemon zest (from about 2 lemons)
- 1 Tbsp vanilla extract
- 1 tsp butter flavoring
- 3/4 c strained fresh orange juice
- 5 large eggs, room temperature

FOR THE SYRUP & GLAZE

- 1/2 c frozen orange juice concentrate, thawed
- 1 Tbsp unsalted butter, melted
- 2 Tbsp dark rum
- 1 c confectioners' sugar divided

Directions

1. Heat the oven to 350°F. Butter and flour a 10-inch tube pan or 12-cup Bundt pan.

2. Sift the flour, sugar, baking powder, and soda into the large bowl of a stand mixer fitted with the paddle attachment. Add the butter and mix on low speed until fine crumbs form.

3. On medium speed, whisk in the oil, lemon zest, vanilla extract, butter flavoring, and orange juice.

4. Whisk in the eggs one at a time and then increase the speed to high and whisk the batter until light, about 3 minutes, scraping the sides of the bowl when needed.

5. Pour the batter into the prepared pan and bake until a toothpick inserted in the cake comes out clean, approximately 45 minutes.

6. To make the syrup and glaze, in a small bowl, mix together orange juice concentrate, butter, rum, and 1/2 cup of the confectioners' sugar.

7. When the cake is done, set the pan on a rack to cool for 5 minutes. With a thin skewer, poke the cake all the way through to the bottom of the pan in about 100 places.

8. Pour 1/3 cup of the syrup over the cake and let it stand for 1 hour before removing it from the pan. (At this point, you can wrap the cake in plastic and hold it for up to 3 days at room temperature; in fact, the flavor only improves.) Cover the remaining syrup with plastic and store at room temperature.

9. When ready to serve, whisk the remaining 1/2 cup confectioners' sugar into the remaining syrup. Set the cake on a rack over a baking sheet and pour the glaze over the cake. Let stand for at least 10 minutes before slicing and serving.

MAKE IT YOUR OWN

5-Star Classic Coconut Cake

INGREDIENTS

- 3 sticks unsalted butter at room temperature, plus more for greasing pans
- 2 c sugar
- 5 extra-large eggs, whisked and at room temperature
- 1 ½ tsp pure vanilla extract
- 1 ½ tsp pure almond extract
- 1 ½ tsp imitation butter flavoring
- 3 c cake flour, plus more for dusting pans
- 1 tsp baking powder
- ½ tsp baking soda
- ½ tsp salt
- 1 c whole milk
- 4 oz sweetened shredded coconut

FOR THE FROSTING

- 1 lb. cream cheese, room temperature
- 2 sticks unsalted butter, room temperature
- ¾ tsp pure vanilla extract
- ¼ tsp pure almond extract
- ¼ tsp imitation butter flavoring
- 1 lb. confectioners' sugar, sifted
- 6 oz sweetened shredded coconut

Directions

1. Preheat oven to 350°F. Grease two 9-inch cake pans and line with parchment or brown paper.
2. Grease the pans again and dust lightly with flour. Discard excess flour.

3. In a large mixing bowl, cream the butter and sugar with an electric mixer on medium-high until light and fluffy – about 5 minutes.

4. Reduce mixer speed slightly and add eggs one at a time, plus vanilla, almond, and butter flavoring. Occasionally scrape sides of bowl while mixing.

5. In another bowl, sift dry ingredients.

6. With the mixer on low speed, alternately add the dry ingredients and the milk to the batter in 3 parts, beginning and ending with the dry ingredients. Mix until well combined. Using a rubber spatula, fold in the 4 ounces of coconut.

7. Pour the batter evenly into the 2 pans and smooth the top with a knife. Bake in the center of the oven for 45 to 55 minutes, until the tops are browned, and the cake tester comes out clean. Cool on a baking rack for 30 minutes, then turn the cakes out onto a baking rack to finish cooling.

For the frosting

- In the bowl of an electric mixer, combine cream cheese, butter, vanilla, and almond extract on low speed. Add the confectioner's sugar and mix until just smooth — do not whip!

- To assemble, place one layer on a flat serving plate upside down and spread with frosting. Place the second layer on top, right side up, and frost the sides and top. Sprinkle the top with coconut and press coconut onto the sides. Serve at room temperature.

MAKE IT YOUR OWN

Kick-To-The-Head Chocolate Cake

INGREDIENTS

- Cooking spray or butter for pan
- 1 ¾ c cake flour, and a dash more for pans
- 2 c sugar
- ¾ c premium unsweetened cocoa powder
- 2 tsp baking soda
- 1 tsp baking powder
- 1 tsp salt
- 1 c buttermilk
- ½ c vegetable oil
- 2 XL eggs, at room temperature
- 1 tsp premium pure vanilla extract
- 1 tsp imitation butter flavoring
- 1 c hot coffee, brewed

ICING

- 6 oz premium semisweet chocolate
- 2 sticks of butter at room temperature
- 1 tsp premium pure vanilla extract
- ½ tsp imitation butter flavoring
- 1XL egg, at room temperature
- 1 ¼ c confectioners' sugar
- 1 tbsp instant coffee crystals

Directions

1. Preheat oven to 350°F. Grease two 8-inch round cake pans, then line with parchment paper. Be sure to butter the paper. Dust pans with flour, shaking out any excess.

2. In a large mixing bowl, mix the flour, sugar, cocoa powder, baking soda, baking powder, and salt on low with an electric mixer.

3. In a medium bowl, stir and combine the buttermilk with the oil, eggs, vanilla, and butter flavoring.

4. Slowly, incorporate the buttermilk mixture into the flour mixture until well combined. Slowly stir in the hot coffee and mix until fully dissolved into the batter.

5. Divide the batter evenly into the prepared pans. Bake for 30 minutes or until a toothpick inserted in the center comes out clean. Remove from the oven and let cakes cool an additional 30 minutes.

6. Flip the cakes upside down on a wire rack to cool completely. Remove the parchment paper from each round.

7. Break chocolate into small pieces in a microwavable bowl and heat in the microwave for 30 seconds. Stir and repeat as often as needed until the chocolate is melted. Stir the completely melted chocolate, then set aside to cool to room temperature.

8. Beat the butter at medium-high speed until pale and fluffy.

9. Add egg, vanilla, and butter flavoring, then beat for at least one minute, being sure to scrape the sides of the bowl to incorporate.

10. With your mixer on low speed, beat in powdered sugar.

11. In a small cup, add coffee, coffee crystals, and 2 tsp of hot water. Slowly mix in the hot coffee and cool chocolate mixture into the butter mixture until all is combined. Do not overbeat.

12. Frost the top of one inverted round. Stack the second round right side up and frost the sides and then the top of the cakes.

MAKE IT YOUR OWN

Toni's Sweet Potato Pie

INGREDIENTS

- 2 ready-made frozen pie crusts, thawed
- 2 large sweet potatoes (about 1 ½ lbs)
- ½ c (1 stick) cold butter, cut into pieces
- 1 ¼ c granulated sugar
- 2 large eggs, room temperature
- ½ tsp ground allspice
- 1 tsp ground cinnamon
- ½ tsp freshly ground nutmeg
- 1 tsp pure vanilla extract
- ½ c orange or mango juice, half
- ¼ c bourbon, optional
- ½ Tbsp lemon juice

Directions

1. Wash the potatoes. In a large saucepan, add the potatoes, half the juice, and cover with water. Bring to a boil and cook on medium-high until soft, approximately 30 minutes.
2. Remove the potatoes from the water and allow to cool. Peel the potatoes, cut, and set them aside.
3. Preheat oven and a baking sheet to 350°F.
4. Puncture pie shells in the center, sit them on the hot baking sheet and par-bake for approximately 15 minutes. Remove and set aside.
5. Add the remaining ingredients and use a mixer to combine, then continue mixing until desired smoothness.
6. Fill the par-baked pie crust 2/3 full and place it on the hot baking sheet and into the oven.
7. Bake for about 35-45 minutes or until a knife inserted in the center comes out clean.
8. Once removed from the oven, brush butter on the browned crust.

MAKE IT YOUR OWN

Red Velvet Cake

I received this recipe from an ex-co-worker. She brought it to work for a Christmas party, and I enjoyed it. It was better and simpler than the recipe I was using. Thanks for sharing the recipe, my friend.

INGREDIENTS

- 1 box Butter Recipe Cake Mix
- 1 tsp cocoa powder
- 1 tsp vanilla extract
- 1 c buttermilk
- 1 bottle red food coloring
- 1 stick of margarine
- 3 eggs
- 1 tsp baking soda
- 1 tsp vinegar

FROSTING

- 8 oz cream cheese
- 1 box confectioner's sugar
- 1 stick margarine
- 1 c chopped pecans
- 1-2 Tbsp. of milk, if needed

Directions

1. Preheat oven to 375°F. Oil and flour three 8" cake pans.
2. Mix the cocoa and cake mix together.
3. Add vanilla, buttermilk, food coloring, margarine, and eggs. Stir until well moistened.
4. Add baking soda and vinegar into the cake mixture.
5. Mix on medium speed for 4 minutes.

6. Pour equal amounts of the batter into the prepared cake pans.

7. Bake in the center of the oven for 25-30 minutes. Remove from oven.

8. While cakes cool, in a medium bowl, mix cream cheese and margarine until smooth. Add sugar a little at a time (with milk if needed) until it's easy to spread. Once cakes cool completely, frost each layer and assemble them on top of each other, adding nuts between the layers and topping off the final layer with nuts.

MAKE IT YOUR OWN

7UP Pound Cake

INGREDIENTS

- 1½ c butter, softened
- 5 eggs at room temperature
- 3 c sugar
- 3 c plain flour, sifted
- 1 Tbsp lemon extract
- ¾ c 7UP
- Baker's Joy baking spray

MAKE IT YOUR OWN

Directions

1. Preheat oven to 325°F. Spray a tube pan with baking spray.
2. Combine the butter and sugar, then mix on medium speed until light and fluffy, about 4 minutes.
3. Add the eggs one at a time, mixing after each addition.
4. Add flour.
5. Mix in the lemon extract and 7UP.
6. Pour the batter into the prepared tube pan.
7. Bake for 60-75 minutes, depending on the oven.

"Don't skimp on ingredients. Buy the best you can and cook it like you love the folks that'll eat it." **—Uncle Wade**

Lemon Bars

INGREDIENTS

Layer 1:
- 1 box Duncan Hines Yellow cake mix
- 1 stick of margarine, melted
- 1 egg

Layer 2:
- 8 oz cream cheese, softened
- 1 box confectioner's sugar (save a bit to dust on top).
- 2 eggs
- 2 tsp lemon extract

Directions

1. Preheat oven to 350°F.
2. Mix the first 3 ingredients.
3. Pour the mixture into a 9X13 pan, then press it into the pan.
4. Mix together the cream cheese, confectioner's sugar, 2 eggs, and lemon extract.
5. Once the mixture is well combined, pour it over the cake batter in the pan.
6. Bake for 30 minutes and then remove the pan from the oven.
7. Allow the cake to cool, sprinkle with remaining sugar, and cut it into bars.

MAKE IT YOUR OWN

Classic Sweet Potato Pie

I was never given the recipe for making sweet potato pie. The following is what I adopted from memories of watching my sisters and mother during the holidays. Mom gave me tips like, "Always use canned milk. Use pure butter. Add a little lemon extract." So feel free to make this recipe your own.

INGREDIENTS

- 4 large sweet potatoes
- 1 c sugar
- ½ stick butter
- ¼ c evaporated milk (more if needed)
- 1 tsp nutmeg
- 1 tsp cinnamon
- 1/8 tsp cream of tartar
- 1 tsp lemon extract
- 2 frozen pie shells, thawed

Directions

1. Wash the potatoes. Add the potatoes to a heavy pot and fill the pot with enough water to cover the potatoes. Bring it to a boil. When the potatoes are soft all the way through, remove them from the pot, allow them to cool, and remove the peels.
2. With an electric mixer, mix together the potatoes, sugar, and butter.
3. Add the milk to the potatoes.
4. Incorporate all of the other ingredients.
5. Prick the bottom and sides of the pie shells and bake the empty shells according to the package instructions.
6. Allow the crusts to cool, then fill them 2/3 of the way full with the potato mixture.
7. Bake the pies in the preheated oven for 45–60 minutes. After about 30 minutes of baking, check often for doneness.

Red Velvet Cake – The Original Family Recipe

This recipe has been in our family for over 40 years. It is the OG of red velvet cakes. Many times, as a cook, you will have to choose between looks and taste. In full transparency, this is not the prettiest girl at the party, but the taste is second to none. Hope you enjoy!

INGREDIENTS

- 2 ½ c cake flour, sifted
- ½ tsp salt
- 3 Tbsp instant chocolate mix
- ½ c butter
- 2 eggs, room temperature
- 1 ½ c sugar
- 2 (1 oz) bottles of red food coloring
- 1 tsp vanilla extract
- 1 tsp butter flavoring
- 1 c buttermilk
- 1 Tbsp white vinegar
- 1 tsp baking soda

WHITE FROSTING

- 4 Tbsp flour
- 1 c whole milk
- 1 c granulated sugar
- 1 stick butter
- 1 c Crisco or other non-liquid shortening
- 3 tsp vanilla
- ½ tsp butter flavoring
- ¼ tsp salt

Directions

1. Preheat oven to 350°F. Grease and flour two 9-inch cake pans.
2. In a small bowl, mix together the first three ingredients. In a larger mixing bowl, cream the butter and sugar well. Once creamed, add eggs one at a time. Mix well, then add food coloring, vanilla, and butter flavoring.

3. In another small bowl, mix together the buttermilk, vinegar, and baking soda.

4. Now, you should have 3 bowls. Alternate adding the flour mixture and buttermilk mixture into the creamed ingredients. Beat gently after each addition.

5. Evenly divide the cake batter between the two prepared pans. Bake for approximately 30 minutes or until the cakes are done. Do not overbake! Remove from the oven and allow cakes to cool on a wire rack for about 15 minutes. Remove the cakes from the pans and allow them to cool completely on wire racks before attempting to add icing.

frosting:

1. Blend the flour and milk, then cook in a saucepan over medium heat until the mixture cooks to a cream-like consistency. Cool, but do not chill.

2. Cream together the butter and other shortening, then add the final 3 ingredients to the butter mixture.

3. Add the cooked flour mixture to the butter and beat until smooth. Spread the frosting atop each layer of the cake, stack the cakes, and frost all sides.

MAKE IT YOUR OWN

Holiday Chocolate Candy with Nuts

INGREDIENTS

- 1 16oz jar dry roasted peanuts, unsalted
- 1 16oz jar dry roasted peanuts, salted
- 12oz semi-sweet chocolate, chopped
- 4oz bar German chocolate
- 3 lbs white almond bark

MAKE IT YOUR OWN

_____
_____
_____
_____
_____
_____
_____
_____

Directions

1. Layer all of the ingredients in a 4 qt. slow cooker.
2. Cover the slow cooker with the lid.
3. Cook on Low for 3 hours.
4. Do Not Remove the Lid.
5. Turn off the slow cooker and allow to cool slightly.
6. Stir and mix thoroughly.
7. Using a teaspoon, drop the chocolate mixture onto a parchment paper-lined baking sheet. Drop the mixture about 2 inches apart.
8. Allowed to harden.

Hummingbird Cake

This recipe was introduced to me by one of the sisters over 40 years ago. It's an old family favorite, relatively easy to make, and a real crowd-pleaser.

INGREDIENTS

- 3 c all-purpose flour
- 2 c sugar
- 1 tsp cinnamon
- 3 eggs, beaten
- 1 ½ c salad oil
- 1 ½ tsp vanilla extract
- 1 tsp salt
- 1 tsp baking soda
- 1 8oz can crushed pineapples, drained
- 2 c chopped walnuts (divided for cake and icing)
- 2 c chopped overly ripe bananas

FROSTING

- 1 box confectioner's sugar
- ½ c butter
- 8oz cream cheese
- 1 ½ tsp vanilla

Directions

1. Preheat oven to 350°F. Grease and flour three 8-inch cake pans. Set aside.
2. In a large bowl, combine all of the cake ingredients (except 1 c of nuts) and stir with a spoon. Divide the batter evenly between prepared pans and bake for approximately 25-30 minutes or until a wooden toothpick inserted in the center of the cake comes out clean.
3. For frosting, combine the butter and cream cheese and beat until smooth. Add the sugar to the mixture, then the vanilla. Once the cakes are completely cool, frost them and garnish them with the remaining nuts if desired.

Judy's Carrot Cake

INGREDIENTS

- 1 ¾ c sugar
- 1 ¼ c Wesson oil
- 4 eggs at room temperature, beaten
- 2 c all-purpose flour
- 2 tsp baking powder
- 2 tsp baking soda
- 1 tsp salt
- 2 tsp cinnamon
- 3 c carrots, shredded
- ½ c chopped nuts

MAKE IT YOUR OWN

FROSTING

- Large can, crushed pineapples, drained and reserving juice.
- 1 box confectioner's sugar
- ½ stick butter, soften
- 2 tsp vanilla extract
- 1 tsp butter flavoring
- 8oz cream cheese

Directions

1. Preheat oven to 350°F. Grease and flour three 9-inch round cake pans.
2. In a large mixing bowl, cream together the sugar and oil. Add the eggs.
3. In a medium bowl, sift together the flour, baking powder, baking soda, salt, and cinnamon. Combine the dry ingredients into the creamed ingredients. Fold in the carrots and nuts.
4. Evenly divide the batter among the 3 prepared cake pans and bake for 25-30 minutes. Once done, remove

the cakes from each pan and allow them to cool on a wire rack.

5. For frosting, drain the pineapple and reserve some of the juice for the frosting. Cream together the butter and cream cheese. Add vanilla, butter flavoring, and the box of powdered sugar.

6. Add just enough pineapple juice to allow the frosting to spread. Place a small amount of frosting, along with drained pineapple, between layers. Frost the cake with the remaining frosting alone.

MAKE IT YOUR OWN

The Ultimate German Chocolate Cake

INGREDIENTS

- 4oz Baker's German Sweet Baking Chocolate
- ½ c boiling water
- 2 c cake flour
- 1 tsp baking soda
- ¼ tsp salt
- 2 sticks butter, softened
- 2 c sugar
- 4 XL eggs yolks
- 1 tsp vanilla
- 1 c buttermilk
- 4 egg whites

FROSTING

- 12oz can evaporated milk
- 1 ½ c granulated sugar
- 1 ½ stick butter
- 4 egg yolks, slightly beaten
- 1 ½ tsp vanilla
- 1 7oz pkg Baker's Angel Flake Coconut (about 2 1/3 c)
- 1 ½ c chopped pecans

Directions

1. Preheat oven to 350°F. Line the bottom of three 9-inch round cake pans with wax paper.

2. Microwave the chocolate and water in a large microwavable bowl on high for 1 ½ to 2 minutes or until the chocolate is almost melted, stirring halfway through the heating time. Stir until the chocolate is completely melted.

3. In a separate bowl, mix the flour, baking soda, and salt. Set aside. Beat the

> "What recipe? There isn't a recipe." —**Every Auntie Ever**

butter and sugar in a large bowl, using an electric mixer on medium speed until light and fluffy. Add egg yolks, one at a time, mixing well after each addition. Stir in the chocolate mixture and vanilla. Add the flour mixture alternately with buttermilk, beating after each addition until smooth.

4. In another large bowl, beat the egg whites with an electric mixer on high until stiff peaks are formed. Gently stir the beaten egg whites into the batter. Evenly divide the batter between the three prepared pans.

5. Place the pans in the oven and bake for 30 minutes or until each cake springs back when lightly touched in the center. Immediately run a spatula between the cakes and the sides of the pans. Cool for 15 minutes, remove the cakes from the pans. Remove the wax paper. Cool the cakes completely on wire racks.

6. For the frosting, in a large saucepan, stir together the milk, sugar, butter, egg yolks, and vanilla. Stir constantly, cook on medium heat for 12 minutes or until it thickens and is golden brown. Remove from heat.

7. Stir in the coconut and pecans. Cool to room temperature and until it is a spreading consistency.

8. Once cooled, spread the frosting between the cake layers and over the top of the cake.

MAKE IT YOUR OWN

CLOSING LOVE LETTER

My Love,

Now, you are off to a good start. Remember to carry on this legacy of nurturing and healing with food. You're also ready to bring into existence your own story. Make it great; make it life-affirming. As I sit here and think about all the things that I want to share with you, all the things I want you to know, most of all, I want you to know how much Faith and Family have brought you to this point. Treasure each of these memories. Honor the ones who have gone before you and celebrate the ones who are beside you now. Perhaps we didn't get it right every time, but we prayed for, advocated, and championed your cause in ways you may never know. So, when you make the sauce or stir the soup or bake the cake, think of us — the family, the one you were born into, the one you adopted along the way, and know that in all we've done, we did it for you.

To all of you who were introduced to our family through this Love Letter Written in Food, may our recipes be a thread, connecting time, experiences, and people into a garment that covers you, not just in the kitchen but in life. You are protected, you are loved, and you are ready for whatever challenges come your way. I pray on your toughest days that you will find the strength to fight your enemies — those inside and out. And on your best days, you'll have the humility and gratitude to consider just how blessed you are.

Always,
Auntie

www.ingramcontent.com/pod-product-compliance
Lightning Source LLC
Chambersburg PA
CBHW061351010526
44107CB00011B/898